MARY BRADLEY.

G. H. K.

Home Management

Home Management

PHYLLIS DAVIDSON

Senior Lecturer in Home Management,
Battersea Training College
of Domestic Science

✧

LONDON

B. T. BATSFORD LTD

First Published, 1960
Reprinted, 1963

MADE AND PRINTED IN GREAT BRITAIN BY
WILLIAM CLOWES AND SONS LTD, LONDON AND BECCLES
FOR THE PUBLISHERS
B. T. BATSFORD
4 FITZHARDINGE STREET, PORTMAN SQUARE, LONDON W.1

Preface

AT THE PRESENT TIME there is an increasing awareness of the need to build sound family life. Efficiency in home skills cannot of itself be effective in creating a successful home, and, in the modern age, standards of skill must be not lowered but adjusted to changed and changing conditions. For successful adjustment, an understanding of home management is essential, and it must be based on factual knowledge concerning both the home itself and the health and comfort of the family living in it.

The purpose in writing this book has been to express that basic knowledge clearly and concisely, so that it may be grasped easily by all concerned with home making—by those engaged in running the homes of today, by students undergoing college training in domestic subjects, and by future home-makers, as yet in the upper forms of secondary schools, who are offering this subject to an increasing extent for examination. Modern scientific developments have enabled the routine work in a home to be accomplished easily and quickly, leaving time for other pursuits, and the sections in the book concerned with this work have likewise been made brief and simple.

The training of a domestic subjects teacher is many sided, and rightly so, for it is recognised that the wider a student's interests are, the greater will be her personal development and her contribution to society. It seems true to say that, of all the subjects taught in a domestic subjects college, home management should be the one in which the others are consolidated; in it, a student has the opportunity to relate much factual knowledge, amassed through other subjects, to the solution of practical problems in everyday living.

In schools, the interests of many older pupils are directed towards the future running of their own homes. The teaching of home management may at this stage impart much that is valuable for the achievement of stability in those homes.

Contents

CONTENTS

List of Illustrations

Acknowledgment

The Author would like to thank Miss A. V. Crawley B.SC. for kindly reading the manuscript and for her valuable comments.

The Author and Publishers wish to acknowledge their appreciation to the following firms and individuals for permitting the use of the illustrations listed below:

The Editor of *Modern Woman*	37, 38
W. N. Froy and Sons Ltd.	3, 13
Council of Industrial Design	4, 11, 12, 13, 14, 16, 17, 39
The Editor of *The Architect and Building News*	11
Maurice Laing, Heal and Son Ltd., S. Greenwood A.R.I.B.A., and H. M. Mitchell A.R.I.B.A.	4
Smith and Wellstood Ltd.	18
The E.L.M.A. Lighting Bureau	40
The Geigy Co. Ltd.	52, 53, 54, 57
The Controller of Her Majesty's Stationery Office and the Director of the Forest Products Research Laboratory	55, 56, 58, 59
Belling & Co. Ltd.	65 (c)
The Association of Building Technicians and Paul Elek Ltd.	1
The Electrical Development Association	8, 24, 34, 47
The Gas Council	9, 10, 28, 29
The Coal Utilization Council	15, 19, 20, 21, 22, 23, 31, 32
Thermodare (Great Britain)	25
Crittall Manufacturing Co. Ltd.	26, 27
Timber Development Association	35, 36
International Paints Ltd	*Jacket design*

and to William Randell for the line drawings not included above.

Chapter 1

The Structure of the House

A PLEASANT AND WELL-PLANNED HOME, comfortable, convenient, satisfying in appearance and with no irritating features in its design, is a great asset to a family. Although comparatively few people are able to have houses built to their own design, the majority find themselves at some time in their lives in search of fresh accommodation. Housewives faced with this problem will look back with gratitude to a school or college training in domestic science which has included some teaching on houses and the important points to be considered in choosing them.

In different parts of the country it has in the past been customary to build with the materials, including wood and various types of stone, found in the district, and this use of local materials had a unifying effect which was very pleasing. In time wood became scarce, transport became easier, and the use of bricks, made of clay and shale embedded in mortar, gradually superseded that of stone. Much work is carried out nowadays in newer materials, but of the existing houses the majority have been built of brick, pleasant in appearance and with good wearing properties. Each brick overlaps the one below, so that there are no straight joints running upwards; the arrangement of the bricks is called the bond. Most of these houses have been constructed so that the weight of upper floors and roof is carried by the walls.

The foundations of a house are of concrete, a mixture of gravel, sand and cement. Each wall is built on a concrete bed wider than the wall itself, and a further layer of concrete, 4 to 6 inches thick, is spread over the whole site. To prevent damp rising into the house through the parts in contact with the ground, all houses require damp-proof courses, made of slates or specially hard engineering bricks, inserted in the walls not less than 6 inches above ground level. Where the ground floor of the house is to be solid, a damp-proof course of asphalt, either sandwiched between two layers of concrete or laid on top, is necessary, and should be continuous with the damp-proof course in the walls so that moisture cannot rise between them.

Walls are of two types, solid and cavity; the better of these is the cavity wall (Fig. 2), consisting of two layers or skins, $4\frac{1}{2}$ inches each in width, with a 2-inch cavity between; these are joined by wall ties, metal strips spaced at intervals of 36 inches horizontally and 18 inches vertically, and twisted so that water cannot cross from the outer to the inner skin. This prevention of damp is taken into consideration throughout

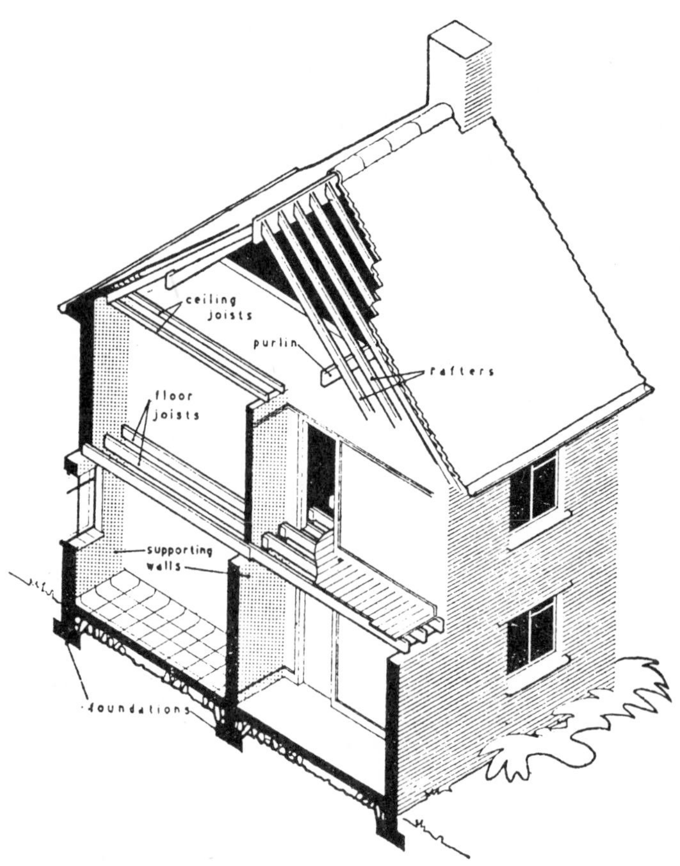

1 *A house with load-bearing walls*

the building of the wall; where the cavity must be bridged around doors and windows, a barrier, usually of bituminous felt, is provided, and further damp-proof materials are used in parapets and chimneys in order to prevent water from the roof from seeping downwards into the building. The inner skin of a cavity wall is often of concrete. Door and window openings are spanned by reinforced concrete lintels which bear the weight of the walls above them.

The floors of a house may be of wood, where boards are laid across joists resting on wall plates, giving a warm resilient flooring, or of concrete, providing a good base for some of the modern floor finishes. Ventilation under the floor area must be provided by building air bricks into the walls, and by resting the joists on small brick sleeper

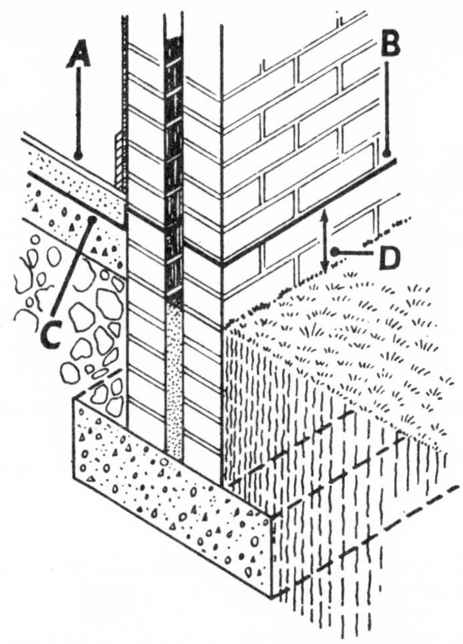

2 *A cavity wall and damp-proof course.* A, *floor finish.* B, *horizontal damp-proof course.* C, "*sandwich*" *damp-proof course in solid floor.* D, 6-*inch minimum*

walls honeycombed to allow the passage of air. Where an adjacent floor is of concrete, pipes are taken through it to enable the air to circulate, a necessary precaution to prevent dry rot from attacking the timber. For floors above ground level, either wood or interlocking pre-cast concrete slabs are used.

The roof which has been most popular in Britain is the pitched or sloping roof made of timber covered with tiles or slates. This gives a space which is useful for storage purposes and for insulating the house against heat and cold, the effect of which can be increased by lining the space with insulating material. The flat roof of concrete is cheaper and is now increasingly used for all types of building.

Framed buildings are now used to a large extent for blocks of flats and offices, and also for houses. Here steel or reinforced concrete beams and columns form a framework designed to carry the entire load of upper floors and roof; and the walling material, used for panels between the columns and beams, does not bear any load.

For all types of building, the use of large building units of concrete has been found to enable walls to be built more quickly than with bricks, and experiments are being made with other materials such as glass, aluminium and plastics. The prefabrication of houses, where large building units are produced in factories and delivered for erection on the site, has been successfully practised in the USA and is being developed in Britain. The method, besides increasing speed of erection, has the advantage of preventing the sections to be used from becoming damp at the site, and of producing better and more comfortable houses; it is likely to be used to a greater extent in the future.

Timber houses, popular in Canada, the USA, Scandinavia and Russia, are being built to an increasing extent in this country; the use of wood has been made possible largely by the import of Canadian timbers. The houses are often built of framed construction. Wood is easy and economical to use, has an attractive appearance and provides excellent insulation. Brickwork, stone and tiles are often combined with the timber and used for external walls to give scope for individuality of design.

The trend in all modern building is to avoid the monotony of some of the past conventional designs and to combine individuality and beauty of appearance with comfort and good use of space.

DAMPNESS

When dampness occurs in a house it may be due to a variety of causes, and since it results in conditions detrimental to health it should never be neglected. A cavity wall, if the necessary damp-proof courses have been efficiently laid, should ensure perfect dryness in the house. If the builder has neglected to keep the cavity clear and has allowed droppings of mortar to collect above the horizontal damp-proof course and form a bridge across the cavity, damp is able to pass from the outer to the inner skin. Where the wall is a solid one, this can of course happen more easily; one wall of the house, owing to the direction of the prevailing wind, may be constantly subjected to rain, and damp patches may occur on the inside. Here the pointing of the brickwork may be discovered to have become defective, and attention to it will remedy the trouble. A waterproof covering applied to the exterior of a solid wall, with the purpose of keeping it damp-proof, often has disappointing results. Rain streaming down the wall may turn in at a crack and soak

3 *A modern bathroom*

4 *The living space in a modern open-plan house*

it; owing to the impervious surface the wall is then unable to dry out by evaporation to the outside, and dampness inside results. A type of rendering which is not liable to crack is the most useful, and careful choice is therefore necessary.

Dry rot is the name given to a condition in wood caused by a fungus which feeds upon it and flourishes in the presence of moisture. Strands called mycelium are thrown out and travel through the wood in all directions; they can even penetrate through brick walls from one area of timber to another. The fungus (Fig. 59) produces fruit bodies, and the millions of spores from these, when carried to a place of favourable conditions, will develop and extend the disease rapidly. The conditions which produce dry rot are the presence of more than 20 per cent water in the wood, together with favourable temperature. In addition to the penetration of damp into the house from outside it, a constantly leaking pipe or dripping tap, causing water to seep down behind some plumbing fixture and reach an area of wood, may cause the fungus to become established. Floor boards, as has been said, must always be thoroughly ventilated from below; the air bricks must never be blocked up from outside. Flower beds must not be built up higher than the level of the damp-proof course; a floor covering such as linoleum, rubber or thermoplastic tiles should never be laid on a damp wood floor. Where the disease is discovered in a house, expert advice should be taken. In bad cases, all the defective wood must be cut away completely, and the remaining area treated with a sterilising liquid; new wood should be similarly treated. Wood which has been attacked has an unpleasant musty smell and a dry crumbling texture into which it is possible to insert a knife easily, with occasional traces of fine red dust of the fungus spores. The dry rot fungus has a natural use. Trees which fall in a wood are destroyed by its action; if this were not to happen, the ground would in time become covered until there was no room for seeds to be fertilised. The rotted wood gives nourishment to the soil.

INSULATION

The purpose of thermal insulation is to ensure that heat does not pass too rapidly from a house in winter, and that in very hot weather the house may remain comparatively cool. The insulating value of all materials used in house construction is now known, and the comfort and economy of good insulation should be a feature of all new houses. Since air is a bad conductor of heat, the air space provided by a pitched roof helps to insulate, but unless further measures are taken, warmth reaching this space will inevitably be wasted. A loose-fill insulating material may be poured and spread between the ceiling joists;

insulating quilts or blankets may be obtained for laying between or over joists; aluminium foil is supplied in rolls 2 feet wide, either with a backing of building paper or with another layer of aluminium, in the latter case one layer being corrugated; this, when laid over ceiling joists with the foil face or corrugated side downwards, forms an air space between it and the ceiling which provides good insulation. The substitution of light-weight concrete blocks instead of bricks for the inner leaf of a cavity wall assists insulation; this material is porous and traps air. A solid concrete floor causes less loss of heat than a suspended wood floor, but the insulation of a suspended timber floor is greatly improved by fixing insulating material below it over the floor joists. The floor area can also be covered with insulating fibreboard, though care must be taken to ensure that dry rot will not develop through inadequate ventilation.

The double glazing of windows, used extensively abroad in colder climates, has not been adopted in this country to any extent, but light inner windows which are easily removable may be fitted to existing frames and can reduce heat loss by as much as 50 per cent. Windows and doors may be fitted with draught-excluding strips of felt, rubber or metal, and this will help to reduce heating costs. The gap at the bottom of the outside door may be closed by nailing a timber fillet to the floor. Another type of draught excluder rises clear of the floor automatically when the door is opened, and this is useful both for outer doors and living-room doors.

Floor boards are sources of draught where no measures have been taken to prevent this, and the air blowing up through the gaps between the boards deposits dust which often appears in unsightly ridges along the floor covering. It is possible to fill the gaps with papier mâché, made by reducing newspaper to pulp in water containing size, and squeezing the surplus water out; the pulp is then pushed well into the cracks with an old knife and left to dry; if desired, it may be stained.

Sound insulation is aimed at preventing noise passing through the partition walls of houses or flats, and at present, owing to the complexity of the problem, the cost of this is high. Even where, because of keeping down costs, no constructional methods are employed, careful positioning of the rooms of houses can do much to lessen the disturbance. The commonest source of annoyance and irritation is the loudspeaker of a wireless or television set in a neighbouring house or flat. Cavity partition walls built between semi-detached or terrace houses, or between flats, assist sound insulation, but in warm weather, when windows are open, there is no remedy against this nuisance except consideration on the part of the neighbours.

EXTERIOR FINISHES

The outside of the walls of a house may be finished in a variety of ways, the purpose being both for decoration and for assisting in weather resistance. Various types of rendered finishes are popular, some of the best known being pebble-dash, where small pebbles are applied to a coat of mortar; roughcast, where the final coat of mortar is coarse in texture and left rough; and textured finishes produced by treating the final coat with tools in order to obtain a pattern. The choice of finish is a matter of personal preference; but, before deciding, it is advisable to consider the probable effects of weathering, or of town atmosphere, which may spoil the appearance in a short time. Both pebble-dash and roughcast are known to wear well. Finishing with a suitable distemper gives a pleasant, fresh appearance when it is newly done, but in a smoky atmosphere it quickly becomes dirty. Various types of emulsion paint for exterior use are more expensive, but more durable. For the exterior woodwork, the use of a good quality glossy paint gives the most durable finish.

INTERIOR FINISHES

The finish which has been most frequently used for walls and ceilings is plaster, a composition of lime, water and sand, flung while wet onto rough surfaces. This method is inexpensive and provides a jointless surface which is hygienic, but the fact that it takes some time to dry out causes delay in the final decoration of the walls. For this reason other materials, including plasterboard, hardboard, plywood and various synthetic plastics, are now often substituted; they can be made in factories and applied dry. For kitchens and bathrooms the most successful wall finish is of tiles—ceramic, glass or plastic. As these are expensive, they are often used to cover half the wall only.

The cheapest, and therefore most often used, finish for walls and ceilings has been distemper, the simple size-bound variety suitable only for ceilings, and the oil-bound or washable distemper known as water paint. This is available in a variety of good colours, is easily renewed when necessary, stands light washing and gives satisfactory wear except in places where steam, which causes it to flake, is produced. Its use has been largely superseded by that of the various emulsion paints; these are based on synthetic resins, and give a tougher surface which will stand up to harder washing. They are available in a large variety of attractive shades and are easily applied to suitable surfaces, the best being dry, firm, slightly porous and free from grease; surfaces which are successful are brick, plaster, plasterboard and similar materials. For redecoration purposes, emulsion paints may be put over wallpaper which is in good condition, and over old oil paint, oil-bound distemper or emulsion paint, provided these are sound; it will not, however, adhere to glossy surfaces unless the gloss is removed by thorough rubbing down, or a special keying solution to assist adhesion is applied. The emulsion paint is thinned either with water or with a special thinning solution supplied by the manufacturers, but too much thinning reduces its covering capacity. It is applied with a distemper brush or varnishing brush 4 to 6 inches wide, or with a paint roller; two coats are nearly always necessary, and as the paint dries very rapidly they can usually be applied in one day. The surface becomes resistant to washing in a few days. The typical paint smell, which many people find trying, is absent. Although certain emulsion paints are specifically recommended for use in kitchens or bathrooms, others are unsuitable, since they absorb moisture, and will not be sufficiently resistant to the frequent soaking and drying out again to which they will be subjected.

Oil-based paints now usually contain resins which impart varying degrees of gloss and wearing quality; these are thinned if necessary with turpentine or turpentine substitute, and can be successfully applied to most surfaces; the majority require undercoating, though some modern paints are said to have such good covering capacity that only the finishing coat is necessary. These paints are suitable for woodwork inside the house, and for both walls and woodwork in kitchens and bathrooms, where a surface which will stand up to heat, condensation, possible splashing and frequent washing is essential. The glossy paints wear best, but have the disadvantage of showing condensation, and therefore paints with low gloss are often preferable, especially for ceilings.

A type of glossy paint requiring only one coat has a jelly consistency and requires no mixing or stirring, being obtainable in tubes ready for use and applied without dripping or splashing; it has good covering capacity, dries quickly and is heat-resistant. Other paints, both finishes and undercoat, have been based on chlorinated rubber and are water resistant, though they are not suitable for use where high temperatures are reached; again, other paints incorporate silicone resins and give good protection against heat and moisture. In the manufacture of all paints the aim is to provide durable coverings which are quickly and easily applied by an amateur. As a result of this, many householders undertake the interior and exterior decoration of their own homes successfully, and where possible some practice should be provided for domestic science students in training, and for pupils in schools with home management flats.

The use of wallpaper has remained very popular; it provides a pleasant wall covering giving scope for much variety in the house, and it is warmer in appearance than any of the various painted surfaces. New types of paste have simplified the hanging of wallpaper, and when a good quality paper is chosen a little practice will enable an amateur to get very satisfactory results. The chief disadvantage is that it is less easily renewed than paint; when redecoration becomes necessary, the old paper should be stripped, a tedious process which is, however, simplified by the use of a suitable stripper.

Chapter 2

Services

WATER SUPPLY

That all houses should have a piped water supply is now taken for granted, and in time to come its lack in some country districts will be remedied, and the system used to supply water to town houses will be extended to cover the whole country.

Rainfall, which forms the source of all our water supply, is collected in various ways in different districts by pumping water directly from a river, by sinking wells to reach the underground natural reservoirs formed where rainwater, soaking into the earth, has encountered an impermeable layer of rock, and by building dams in hilly districts and conveying water through pipes to service reservoirs, from which it may flow by gravity to where it is required. Before entering the main pipes which convey it to a town, the water must undergo purification treatment, filtration and chlorination, in order to remove suspended impurities and to sterilise it; the water which finally reaches the householder can therefore be guaranteed to be non-injurious to health. Since it is one of the most essential services, a householder should understand clearly the arrangement of service pipes, precautions to be taken against freezing, and the points on which depends the efficiency of the appliances forming part of the system.

Close to the place where the cold water from the main supply is conveyed into the house in a service pipe under pressure, there is a stop tap for the householder's use. Before the service pipe rises to the storage tank, branch pipes are taken from it to any points in the house where drinking water is required. Although the practice in many houses has been to confine this supply of drinking water to the tap at the kitchen sink, it is obviously more convenient if all cold water taps in the house are supplied with water from the mains and therefore fit for drinking.

The storage tank must be placed at the highest point in the system, so that when a tap is turned on there will be sufficient pressure to cause the water to flow. For this reason, and also to have it conveniently out of the way, the tank in many houses is in the loft, where in very cold weather the temperature drops considerably and, unless careful insulation has been carried out, freezing and burst pipes may result. Furthermore, the loft is often difficult of access, and a better practice is to place the storage tank above the hot-water cylinder in the upper part of an airing cupboard, or somewhere near a flue or warm-air duct. The tank should always be covered.

The flow of water into the cold storage tank is controlled by a ball valve. Connected to the inlet is a metal rod, at the other end of which is attached a hollow metal ball which floats on the water. When the tank is full, the ball has risen to such a position that the opening of the inlet pipe is closed by a stopper at the end of the rod; when water is

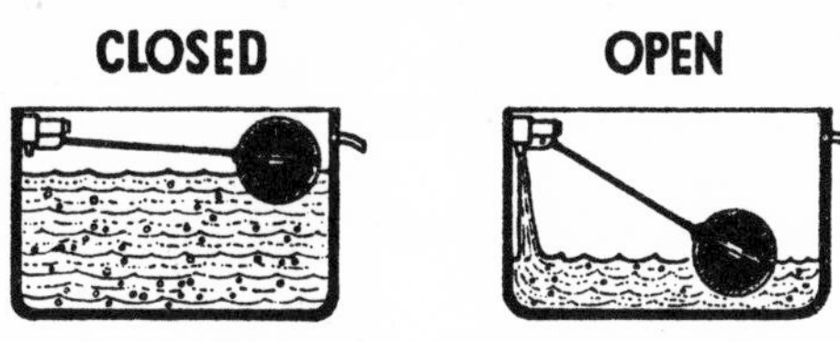

5 *A ball valve: closed and open*

drawn from the tank and the level falls, the ball falls with it, pulling out the stopper and allowing fresh cold water to enter. An overflow pipe is taken from the tank, about 1 inch above the level of the water when the tank is full, to the outside of the house, a precaution against any defect developing in the ball valve control. From the storage tank supply pipes lead to any cold-water taps which have not been fed from the mains, to the W.C. cistern, and to the hot-water storage cylinder, where it enters at the bottom.

The size of the hot-water cylinder must be adequate for the requirements of the household; for a family of four, a cylinder of 25 gallons capacity is usually adequate provided there is an efficient water-heating system which will maintain a temperature of 140° Fahrenheit. The cylinder should be in a vertical position, and its height at least twice its diameter; to prevent heat loss it should be insulated.

Details of the various ways of heating water will be given under separate headings; for the purpose of understanding the circulation of hot water it will be simplest at this stage to imagine that the heat is supplied by a boiler situated, at a lower level than the cylinder, in the kitchen or utility room, or by a back boiler.

The boiler is supplied with cold water from the bottom of the cylinder; as it is heated, it rises by convection through a pipe which enters the cylinder at a point near to the top, and cold water flows into the boiler to take its place. Correct arrangement of pipes in boiler and cylinder is important in order to avoid undue mixing of the hot and cold water. As convection currents continue, the hottest water will

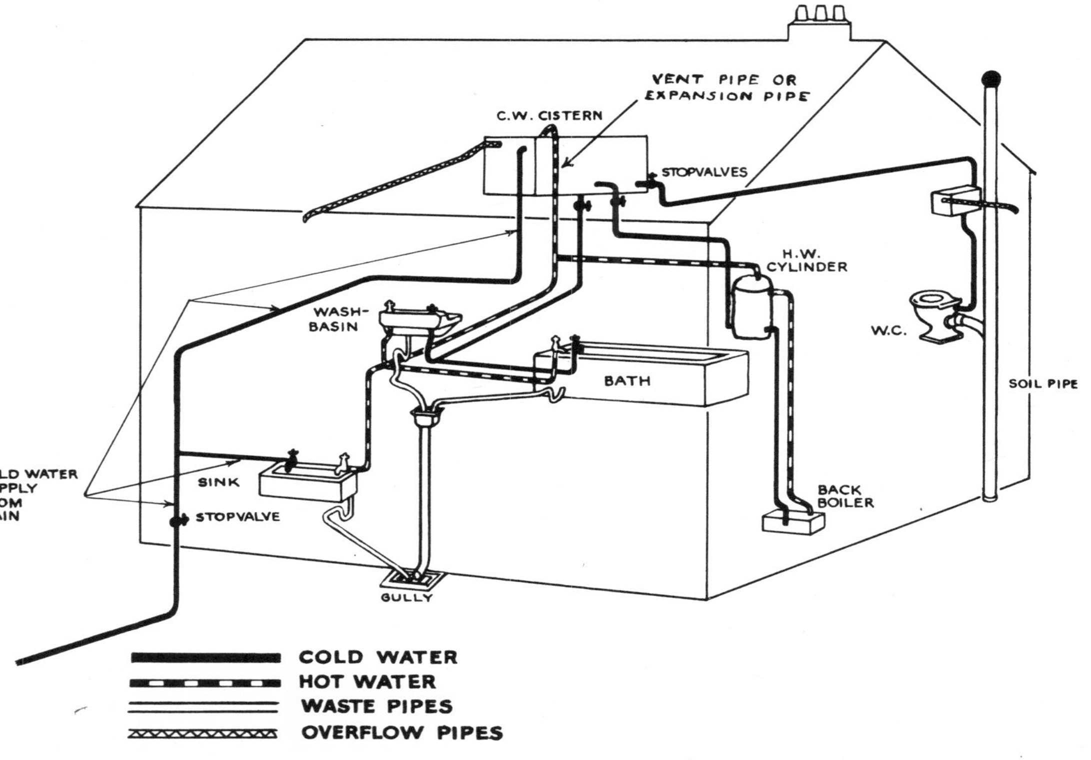

6 *Hot and cold water circulation in a house*

collect at the top of the cylinder; in time, if none is drawn off from the taps, the cylinder will become full of hot water.

From the top of the cylinder a pipe leads off to a point above the cold storage tank, where it is open at the end for the escape of steam; this is called the vent pipe or expansion pipe. Should the water begin to boil, it will rise up this pipe and overflow into the cold tank. When, as in many older systems, the vent pipe rises vertically, directly from the top of the cylinder, one-pipe circulation will occur; the rising hot water will meet the cold sides of the vent pipe and begin to trickle back into the cylinder, causing some loss of heat; this should be avoided, particularly where an immersion heater is used for any part of the year. Therefore, the vent pipe should, upon leaving the cylinder, run horizontally for about 18 inches before rising vertically.

Hot-water supply pipes lead off to the various hot taps in the house, in kitchen, bathroom, cloakroom and possibly bedrooms. When one of these taps is turned on, cold water will immediately enter the bottom of the cylinder from the storage tank, by its pressure forcing the hot water from the top of the cylinder out of the tap. In the cold tank the ball valve will operate, allowing fresh water from the main supply to enter the tank.

Whatever the fuel used, all service pipes should be as short as possible to avoid waste of heat, and in modern houses the plumbing is confined to a small section and pipes are never spread out unnecessarily over the house.

Since it is undesirable, especially in hard-water districts, for the water to boil, in a solid fuel system without thermostatic control it is an advantage to run a towel rail or radiator from the system, just above the boiler, in order to use surplus heat. It should, of course, be possible to disconnect it in the summer months when an immersion heater may be in use.

DRAINAGE

As in the case of the piped water supply, there is great need for modern drainage systems to be extended over the country as a whole, and for the elimination of the primitive methods which exist in some rural areas.

In the system of house drainage most commonly used in this country, the waste from sinks, wash basins and baths is conveyed through the walls to the outside of the house by pipes which discharge it into gulleys, and from there it flows into drain pipes; rainwater collecting in roof gutters is similarly discharged. Gulleys must be kept clean and free from leaves. W.C. waste is conveyed away by a soil pipe leading directly to the underground drain; this pipe is carried upwards to a point well above the highest window or ventilator in the house, where it is open to provide an outlet vent for the drain; the wire cage which covers the opening must be kept free from obstruction. The underground drain

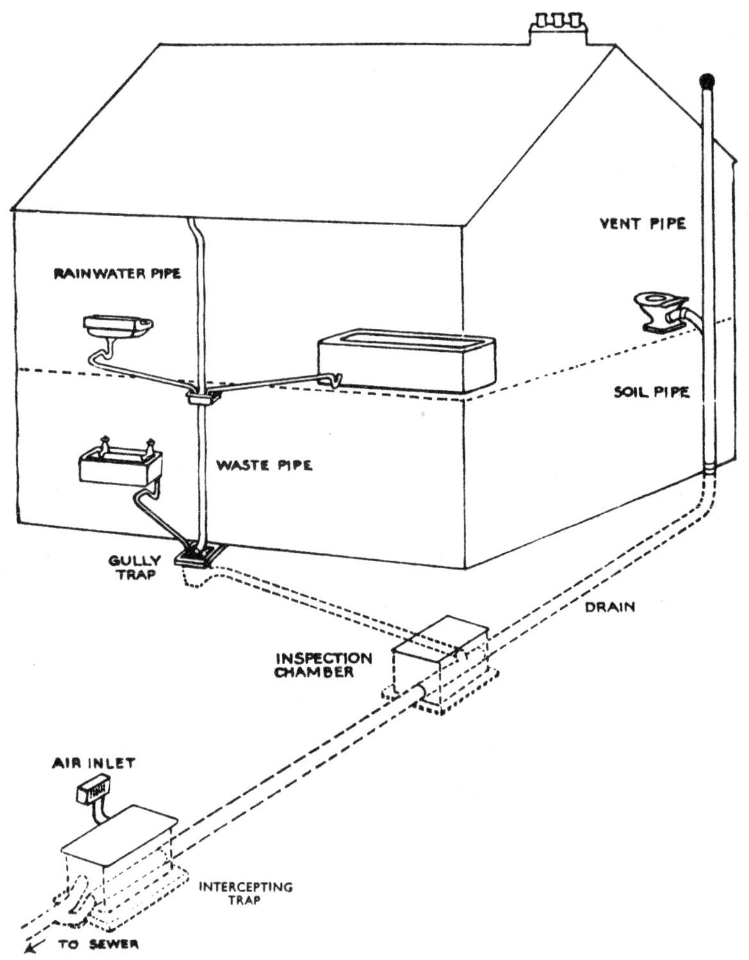

7 *Drainage of a house*

has also an inlet vent, at some distance from the house. This arrangement has the two disadvantages of several unsightly pipes being visible on the outside of the house, and of the risk of outside pipes freezing in winter; the better system is the more modern "one pipe" method, whereby all waste is directed into one common pipe, also carried up above the roof for the purpose of ventilation, and enclosed in a duct in the wall of the house, accessible from inside, to prevent freezing.

Each appliance connected with the drainage of the house is provided with a trap or U bend in the waste pipe, where clean cold water collects and acts as a seal to prevent any foul air rising into the house from the drain. Where individual house drains join on their way to the street sewer, manholes are provided so that inspection and cleaning may take place when necessary. The street sewer in its turn joins the main sewer, which conveys the waste away from the town.

A modern sewage plant is built, when possible, at a lower level than the town it serves, so that the sewage may flow by gravity to the works, and the expense of pumping it be kept to a minimum. At the sewage works it undergoes various chemical and bacteriological treatments, which purify the effluent and convert the solids into fertiliser which can be dried and sold to farmers. The effluent is rendered harmless and fit for discharge into rivers. Methane gas formed during the process may be used to drive the machinery of the plant.

Other methods of sewage disposal are practised in different parts of the country. The sewage may be discharged into the sea, where mixing with sufficient quantity renders it harmless, or it may be fed to the soil in sewage farms where, under right conditions, the liquid is drained away and the solids are collected on the surface as manure. The modern scientific treatment is preferable to these.

SANITARY FITTINGS

Much advance has been made in the design of sanitary fittings (Fig. 3). Baths are usually of cast iron, covered with porcelain of good quality which is no longer liable to chip or discolour; they are built-in, with panels of smooth material hiding pipes and facilitating cleaning. Wash basins in porcelain, stainless metal or plastic are often of the pedestal type, so that the waste pipe is concealed. Taps are of stainless metal and smooth design, and should be fitted so that corners awkward for cleaning are eliminated. Splash-backs are of tiles or plastic or other easily cleaned material. Water closets are usually made of vitreous china, with plastic and chromium fittings; the low suite is the most popular variety, eliminating exposed pipes, and operating efficiently and quietly by a lever or push button.

Modern kitchen sinks are of glazed earthenware, porcelain enamel of improved quality, stainless steel or other metal, or plastic. It is an advantage to avoid dirt traps by having draining boards made in one piece with the sink; where wooden boards are preferred they should be removable.

ELECTRICITY

There are certain basic facts about the supply of electricity to a house which the householder should understand in order to use it intelligently and ensure that the appliances are kept in efficient working order.

Electricity is conveyed into a house by a cable containing two wires, the red or live wire, and the black or neutral wire. *Direct current*, as its name implies, flows continuously through the wires in one direction, while *alternating current*, now used in most installations and eventually to be universal, changes direction. The wires pass first through the electricity company's fuse box, which the householder must not interfere with, and then through a meter where the current used is recorded; the main circuit is then split into sections, each with its own fuse box. From each of these, cables run to the different circuits. In the ring circuit, a modern type of installation, cables run to one point and on from it to the next, until all the points have been served, finally returning to the starting place; in this system, a very convenient one, all appliances have plugs of 13 amps, each plug having its own fuse suitable for the apparatus to which it is connected.

A fuse is a safety device in the form of a thin piece of wire which is a part of the circuit; it melts or breaks as a result of overloading the circuit or through a fault developing in it. Without this safety measure, overheating of cables could cause fire. The replacement of fuse wire is a simple process which a householder should be able to do, bearing in mind that the correct thickness of wire must be used for the particular circuit. As a general rule, the melting of the fuse is an indication of a fault needing attention, and this should be discovered and remedied; occasionally, however, a fuse wire melts through deterioration in the wire itself.

Cables are covered in lead or thick rubber, and are usually embedded in walls or under floors. Flexible wires must be of suitable thickness for the appliances they serve; each conductor is insulated with rubber and, where the flex is for lighting, has an outer covering of cotton or plastic; for appliances such as suction cleaners, irons and heaters the flex is sheathed in stout rubber which will stand the wear of constant movement.

Home accidents arising from the use of electrical appliances are rare; nevertheless, the conditions which may cause electric shock should be understood. If through the breakdown of insulation the metal frame of an appliance should, by contact with a live wire, itself become live, anyone touching it will experience shock, caused by the uncontrolled current trying to return to earth and finding a path through the body. The shock may be very slight; if, however, the person is standing on a damp concrete floor, or touching anything else in contact with earth, it may be severe, or even fatal. All apparatus should therefore be earthed; a 3-pin plug and 3-wire flex should be used, and the third wire, usually coloured green, connected to the earth pin. In modern installations, all plug suckets are 3-pin, and 2-wire flex is used for lights and small appliances only. A further safety measure may be provided with shutters dropping over the live and neutral sockets and lifted only by the insertion of the earth pin; this prevents a child from inserting anything into the sockets and touching live wires.

Except in the case of the ring circuit, the size of plug and socket fitted for any appliance is governed by the quantity of electricity flowing through it, which is measured in amperes. This may be determined by dividing the wattage, marked on the appliance, by the voltage. A 1000-watt kettle on 250 volts will require a 5-amp plug; a 2-bar fire, 2000 watts, will require a 15-amp plug.

Failure of a piece of electrical apparatus is most often caused by a fault in the flex, either close to the plug terminals or to where it is connected with the apparatus. Insulation should be regularly inspected for signs of fraying; repairs and renewals should be attended to immediately they become necessary, but only by someone who fully understands them, preferably a qualified electrician.

Payment for Electricity

The unit used as the basis of payment is the *kilowatt hour*—1000 watts running for one hour. Various methods of payment are adopted by different companies, some of which offer a choice to new consumers. Examples of these are:

Flat Rate Here several rates are used according to whether the current is used for lighting, heating or water heating.

Variable Block Tariff A fixed number or block of units used in each quarter is charged at a comparatively high rate, based on the size of the house; the remaining units used are charged at a lower rate.

Two-part Tariff A fixed charge is made per quarter; in addition, all units are charged at a relatively low rate. It should be remembered that the payment made is for a complete service. Since electricity cannot be stored, the production plant must be large enough to supply the maximum quantity demanded at peak periods. From this it follows that customers should be encouraged to use electricity as much as possible in the off-peak periods, and tariffs are designed with this end in view.

Reading the Electricity Meter

A meter is easy to read if these simple rules are followed. The dials register thousands, hundreds, tens and single units (kilowatt hours or kWh.). The dials registering tenths and hundredths of a unit (figures sometimes red instead of black) may be disregarded, as they are used mainly for testing purposes. The hands in adjacent dials revolve in opposite directions. Begin reading at the left-hand dial. When the hand is between two figures write down the lower figure. When the hand is between 0 and 9, always write down 9. Go through the same process with the other dials, writing down the figures in the order left to right, remembering that when the hand is *between* two figures always write

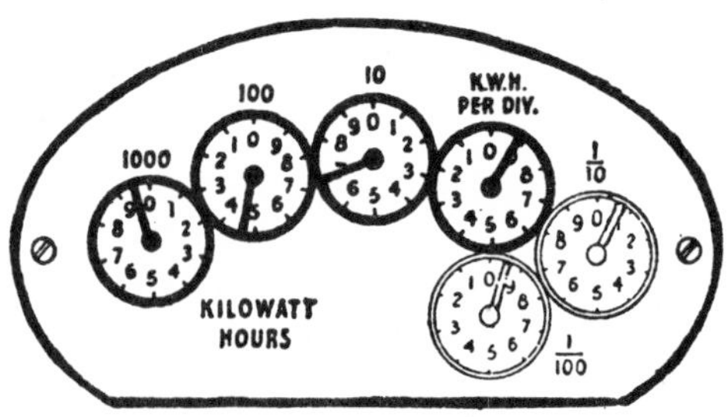

8 *Electricity meter dials*

down the lower figure. When the hand is *on* a figure (say 7) you write down 6 (not 7) unless the hand on the next dial on the right is between 0 and 1. In Fig. 8 the reading of the meter is 9469 units. It is worth while keeping a record of the figure on the meter card usually supplied by the electricity authority.

GAS

The gas which is used in the home for cooking, space heating, water heating and refrigeration is a product of the carbonisation of coal. During the process, the gas is given different purifying treatments, in the course of which many useful by-products are produced; examples of these are antiseptics, fuel oils, dyes and many other valuable chemicals. The gas is stored in large holders, and from these is sent out through main street pipes, with smaller branch pipes leading to individual houses. The distinctive smell of gas is not disguised in any way, so that leaks may easily be detected. The gas supply to a house may be turned off by a control tap placed beside the meter. In the meter it is measured in cubic feet.

Payment for Gas

In different parts of the country, there are slight variations in the heating power of gas; payment must therefore be made for the amount of heat produced and not for the cubic feet consumed. The heat produced is calculated in *British Thermal Units*; a British Thermal Unit is the amount of heat required to raise the temperature of 1 pound of water through 1 degree Fahrenheit; 100,000 British Thermal Units are the equivalent of 1 *therm*. The heating power or calorific value of gas means the number of B.Th.Us. obtained from 1 cubic foot of gas, the average for the country being 500. When the meter reading is taken, the number of cubic feet used since the last reading is noted, and multiplied by the calorific value. The result is reduced to therms by dividing by 100,000, and payment is made per therm.

Reading the Gas Meter

There are four main dials, with one additional smaller dial (or sometimes two, as in Fig. 9) for testing purposes. The reading is taken as for the electric meter, but as the right-hand dial registers hundreds, 00 must in this case be added to the figures read.

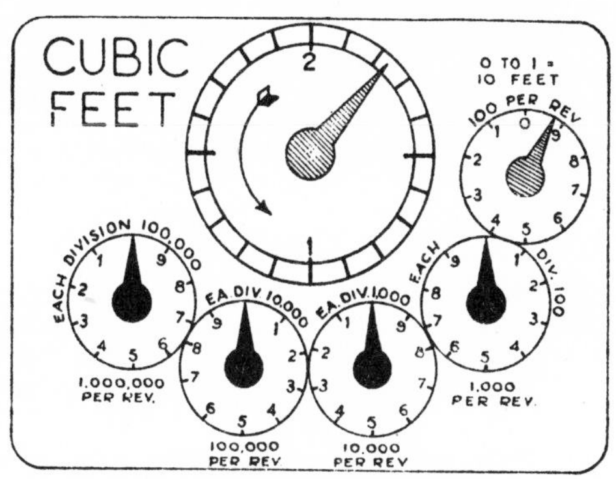

9 *Gas meter dials*

THERMOSTATIC CONTROL OF ELECTRICITY AND GAS

The thermostat is a device used to control the supply of electric current, or of gas, in order to maintain a predetermined temperature; it is fitted to many appliances for heating, water heating and cooking. A simple type of thermostat on electric appliances consists of a bi-metal strip; when heated, this will bend, and in doing so will open the contact and disconnect the current. As the temperature falls, the strip resumes its former position and the current is switched on. In this way a constant temperature may be maintained and wastage of electricity avoided.

A commonly used gas thermostat (Fig. 10) consists of a steel rod **B** enclosed in a brass tube **A** and attached at one end to the brass and at the other end to a valve **C** controlling the supply of gas. When heated, the brass tube expands more than the steel, and carries the rod along with it, thereby bringing the rod closer to the seating **S**, reducing the supply of gas; upon cooling, the procedure is reversed. A cooker thermostat is adjustable by a knob and dial fitted to the outside; the turning of the knob alters the position of the valve in order to maintain the temperature desired.

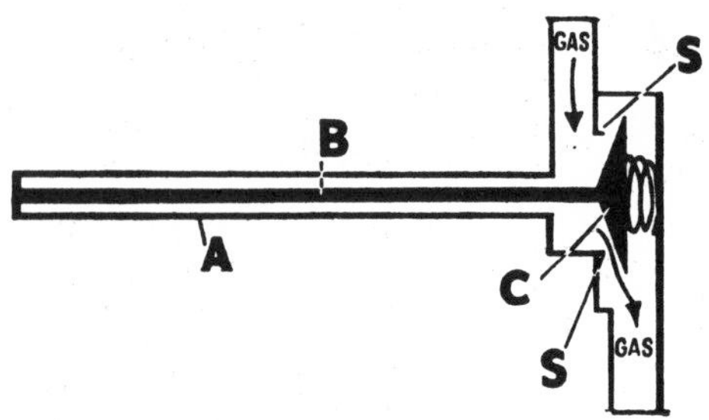

10 *A gas thermostat*

11 *The living-room in a modern semi-detached house*

12 *A well-designed kitchen*

Chapter 3

The Arrangement of Space

TOO MANY EXISTING HOUSES have been planned without sufficient foresight and prove to be inconvenient in use. Much research on house design has taken place, and is continuing, so that in the future houses will be produced in which economy in building will be combined with comfort, convenience and a sense of space.

The minimum amount of space for a family of four—parents and two children of opposite sex—was stated in 1944 to be 900 square feet. Houses which are too small provide endless irritations, and now it is often accepted that the minimum size for this family should be 1000 square feet. It is also true that a well-designed and well-run home can help to maintain the health of the family by preventing the frustrations and consequent neuroses which often arise from inadequate and inconvenient surroundings.

For most people the first and most important consideration will be the planning of the living space; here the family will spend most time together, relaxing, carrying out leisure activities and entertaining their friends (Fig. 4). The last point is an important one, for to be able to invite friends into comfortable surroundings, and entertain them to meals without causing irritation or inconvenience, adds greatly to the satisfaction of having a home, and contributes much to the contentment of the family, and especially that of the young people in it. The living-room should be large enough to hold easily the furniture necessary for the comfort of the family and occasional visitors, without looking or feeling overcrowded. It should be light, with if possible a south aspect for the maximum amount of sunshine, and easily warmed. If two doors are necessary, they should be placed in such a position that draughts are avoided, and people crossing from one to the other will not have to make a passage over the living area. Special consideration should be given to making this room as soundproof as possible. Where expense allows, thick solid doors, double windows and special sound-absorbing treatment of the ceiling all help, but at least the position of the room should be planned so that noises from other parts of the house will be diminished.

In this country the provision of a separate meals room, however small, has always been preferred, and from surveys made from time to time it is found to be still popular with the majority. It has obvious advantages. Apart from its use for meals, the additional room is convenient for children doing homework, especially when the rest of the family wish to enjoy wireless or television programmes, and for dress-making or similar types of activity apt to cause untidiness. Where several of the family are working outside the home, meals are often served at different times to different people. When entertaining guests to a meal, it is convenient to leave the clearing of the table until after their departure, more easily achieved when a door can be closed upon it. Even when family meals are for the most part taken in the kitchen, the separate room is much preferred for entertaining, not so much from snobbery as for convenience. The meals room requires some form of heating, intermittent or continuous according to its use, and it entails additional housework, but the saving of fuel and of labour are by no means the most essential factors in securing happy family living.

The provision of one living-room only, however, with space for a dining area, is very suitable where there are no children, and for retired couples (Fig. 11). The most satisfactory design has a dining area which is given some appearance of separation from the living area, and is connected with the kitchen by a door or hatch. Even though there is a separate meals room or a meals area in the living-room, in the majority of houses some meals are eaten in the kitchen, and space should be provided there for this purpose. To make adequate allowance for it, the minimum area of the kitchen for a family of four should be 100 square feet, though 120 square feet is preferable.

THE KITCHEN

Much has been written on the subject of kitchen planning, and the many magazines concerned with the home continue to produce suggestions, mostly excellent, for designing new kitchens and for converting old ones. In either case, certain main considerations should be borne in mind.

The idea held in the past was that the kitchen should face north. With the advent of refrigeration and well-insulated cookers and water heaters, together with the popularity of large windows and venetian blinds, the reasons for this have disappeared, and since meals are eaten in the kitchen and the housewife spends a large proportion of her day in it, an aspect which ensures at least the morning sun is desirable. For the sake of the brief periods of really hot weather which occur in summer, a south-west aspect should be avoided.

The mistake most often made in kitchen design is in the placing of windows and doors so that they take up wall space needed for equipment and cause unnecessary movement and draughts. Housewives sometimes state that they prefer a kitchen to be square, but the rectangle, with doors together at one end and the maximum wall space left for equipment at the other, usually proves the most labour-saving shape. The side at which each door is hinged also needs to be considered; the space between two doors is often suitable for a store cupboard for cleaning materials.

The greatest number of hours spent in a kitchen is concerned with the preparation of meals, and this follows a logical sequence of movement, from the area in which the food is stored to that where it is prepared and cooked, and finally to the washing-up area (Fig. 12). The three chief pieces of equipment—refrigerator, cooker and sink—should therefore be placed in convenient proximity, either along the three walls forming the end of the rectangle, in a U shape, or along two of them, forming an L. Where it fits more conveniently, the sink may be placed in between the preparation and cookery areas (Fig. 13); from the point of view of good lighting, and for the escape of steam, most people prefer it to be beneath a window, though where the window is a good size it is quite satisfactory on the wall adjacent to it. In a small kitchen the provision of two draining boards is unnecessary, though there must be an adequate flat counter space or other working surface, on the side opposite to draining, where dishes to be washed may be stacked. A double sink makes efficient washing up much easier, and is an undoubted advantage where laundrywork is done in the kitchen. Its size often prevents it from fitting in easily.

Much modern kitchen equipment has been made to a standard height of 36 inches, so that appliances and working surfaces form a continuous level. While this is pleasing and efficient in appearance, the standard height has been found by many housewives to be too high for some purposes, except in the case of the sink, where the depth of the bowl lowers the working level. Modern electric cookers 33 inches high can be supplied with a plinth for use when 36 inches is preferred, and this practice may with advantage be extended to all kitchen equipment. It is useful to have one surface, with knee space below, low enough for a housewife to sit at in comfort.

The use of wood for the work surfaces in a kitchen has been superseded by laminated plastic, fixed with adhesive, its edges enclosed by beading. This is obtainable in a variety of colours to fit in with kitchen schemes; it is easily cleaned by wiping over with a cloth wrung out of warm water. It wears very well, though chopping directly onto the surface will scratch it; it will stand a fairly high temperature, but the use of saucepan stands is advisable for pans straight from the cooker. It is a hygienic surface and very suitable for pastry rolling.

The placing of the store cupboards relevant to each working area is of great importance, and forethought here can do much to save unnecessary steps. Adequate working surfaces for the preparation of food should be planned near to the refrigerator, and between the sink and cooker; a further counter or cupboard top on the other side of the cooker, for dishing up a meal, is an advantage; where there is a hatch connected with the meals room, this serving space should be close to it. A two-way cupboard and drawer below it, opened both from dining-room and kitchen, are convenient for the storage of crockery, cutlery and table linen in everyday use. It is also possible to build a storage unit around the hatch. An adequate supply of base store cupboards with working-top surfaces, and wall cupboards reaching to ceiling height to avoid dust traps, is essential in a labour-saving kitchen. When placed directly above base cupboards, wall cupboards should give a clearance of at least 18 inches; for convenience in working, the main preparation surface in the kitchen should have no wall cupboard above it.

Articles in daily use should be easily accessible, while extra things not required regularly may be kept in the "dead" storage space provided by the ceiling-high cupboards. All cupboard shelves should be both wide enough and deep enough to take their contents easily, and the cupboard with adjustable shelves is by far the most practical. A cupboard for dry stores will require a shelf clearance of at least 7 inches and not more than 10 inches; narrow shelves are useful for small articles; very deep shelves are inconvenient and it is difficult to reach to the back. A shelf covering, firmly fixed, should be used for lining; like things should be stored together; jars should be clearly labelled when necessary; tall jars and bottles should be placed at the back. Special shelves for the storage of preserves are useful. Saucepans are best kept on a slatted shelf open to the air and the lids inside a rack fixed to the inner side of a cupboard door.

Modern sink units have various arrangements of cupboards below them to take cleaning materials, buckets and bowls; a receptacle for rubbish is often fitted, an improvement on this being the electric waste-disposal unit capable of disposing of all rubbish except tins. Where a sink with open space below it is preferred, shelves to take equipment should be fitted.

The ideal arrangement for the storage of perishable foods is by means of a refrigerator; the fuel used may be electricity, gas or oil. Refrigerators are made in different sizes, determined by the capacity of the storage cabinet, which is measured in cubic feet of space; it is an

13 *A small labour-saving kitchen*

14 *A kitchen with a meals area and utility room*

advantage to place the refrigerator in a cool part of the kitchen. By the extraction of heat, the interior of the cabinet is kept at a temperature sufficiently low to keep foods fresh for a reasonable period, the length of time depending on the type of food and its degree of freshness when it is put into the refrigerator. Special care is necessary over the storage of fish, poultry and meat, which are more perishable than other foods, and in which bacteria may grow rapidly without being apparent. For general purposes the temperature is best kept at about 40°F. by setting the control knob as directed by the manufacturers. The ice containers should be filled with clean cold water and dried outside before placing in the freezer. Keeping the stored foods covered by wrapping them in grease-proof paper or aluminium foil, or by putting them into plastic bags or containers, will prevent tainting by strongly smelling foods. Milk bottles should be kept covered. Foods requiring the lowest temperature should be placed near the freezer; frozen foods will keep for the longest time inside it, in their packets. The inside of the cabinet should be kept spotlessly clean. During any period when it is out of use, all food should be removed, and the door left open.

Where there is no refrigerator, a cool larder or larder cupboard must be used for the storage of perishables. This should be built on the north side of the house, and be well ventilated but impervious to flies. Walls and floor should be of some cold, smooth and easily cleaned material; tiles are suitable. One shelf at least should be tiled or marbled. Vegetable racks of various designs are available, and one of these is a necessity in most kitchens, though where there is a refrigerator, vegetables should be kept in it as much as possible.

THE MEALS AREA

Where possible, the best arrangement is to have this in a recess; more often, however, it must be planned in the kitchen, making use of any available space (Fig. 14). When in a corner, built-in seats along the two walls are economical of space. When there is no room for a table to stand permanently, a hinged flap may be fixed to a wall or cupboard door, or a breakfast counter may be substituted. If space permits, the meals corner or recess may be screened from the rest of the room; when possible, it should have a window. Upholstered seats should be covered in washable plastic material. The meals table, if covered with laminated plastic, usually provides a useful additional working surface, and also solves the problem of a table for the children's homework.

LAUNDRY FACILITIES

In spite of the growth of launderettes, and the undoubted advantage of sending large articles to a commercial laundry, many housewives for various reasons prefer to do the bulk of their weekly washing and ironing at home, and in all house plans this must therefore be taken into consideration. The ideal arrangement is to build a separate utility room adjacent to the kitchen, fitted with a laundry sink, washing machine, drying equipment and ironing accommodation; storage cupboards for laundry and cleaning materials should also be fitted. Where the utility room is not possible, the equipment must be fitted into the kitchen; fortunately this is made easier by the wide range of sizes available in modern laundry equipment. Further suggestions for the choice of such equipment will be found in Chapter 13.

THE HALL AND STAIRCASE

Many small houses give an immediate impression to anyone entering them of being cramped, and this is often due to the narrowness of the hall. Even a small hall which is square in shape and well lit can be attractive and welcoming to visitors. For the purpose of convenience, the staircase should be placed fairly centrally in the house. The custom, followed in other countries, of placing it in the living-room is unsuitable unless there is adequate central heating; and where there are children, the noise of wireless or television programmes penetrating to bedrooms is a disadvantage. The staircase should be well lit, and have as few turns as possible.

THE BEDROOMS AND BATHROOM

As with all rooms, the bedroom must be designed so that the essential pieces of furniture may be fitted in without difficulty. The bed, if against a wall, should be easily moved out for making; all double bedrooms should be large enough to take two single beds (Figs. 16, 17). Fitted cupboards built to the ceiling should provide adequate shelf and hanging space, the upper sections being useful for such things as reserve blankets. Space for a dressing-table and mirror in good light, and a bedside table, is essential. The best aspect for a bedroom is east or south-east. The bathroom (Fig. 3) should be upstairs, with a heated towel rail and fitted medicine cupboard. Unless there is a downstairs cloakroom with lavatory, the upstairs lavatory should be separate from the bathroom.

STORAGE FACILITIES

A good linen cupboard, warmed and ventilated, with shelves 2 feet deep and at least 2 feet 6 inches wide, is essential. Warmth may be provided by the hot-water storage cylinder, and will be sufficient even when this is well lagged. Should there be no stored hot water, an electric tubular heater will be adequate and economical. The linen cupboard is often situated in the bathroom, not very desirable because of the steamy atmosphere, but giving welcome warmth to the room. In some houses it is placed in a bedroom or on the landing.

Some provision should be made in every house for the storage of trunks and boxes, and here the space made by a pitched roof, provided it is boarded in to ensure dryness, and well ventilated, is valuable; some form of easy access is necessary, and the door leading from a bedroom, possible in some designs, is more convenient than the more usual trap-door.

Adequate storage facilities for solid fuel are essential for a number of reasons. Owing to the improvements in design of all kinds of appliances burning solid fuel, its use is increasing, and every encouragement is given to the public to use it efficiently and economically. Production at the coal-mines continues throughout the whole year, and since it cannot be stored at the mines, it must be sent out to the coal merchants throughout the year, and not only when it is most in demand. Inducement is given to customers to purchase it during the summer months by a slight lowering of prices for a short period; unfortunately, inadequate storage space prevents many from complying. Smokeless fuels (now in increasingly wide use in the many new appliances designed to burn them) require considerably more storage space, as they are less dense than bituminous coal, and this creates additional difficulty, especially in small houses.

Ideally, all houses should have a fuel store capable of holding two types of fuel, and adequate for the entire winter's supply. It should be conveniently near to the house, and approached under cover, but not in such a position that coal dust can penetrate to the living area. The coal bunker built against the wall of a house, which can be supplied from outside and extracted from inside, is very convenient, but inevitably causes some coal dust in the house. Careful attention should be paid to the design of the extraction opening. Where there is a door to the bunker, removable boards fitted into grooves inside it are usually necessary, to prevent coals from falling into the kitchen when the bunker is full; a hatch opening, together with a carefully sloped floor, may be designed so as to make this unnecessary. For the sake of appearance, coal bunkers are usually built in brick or concrete to match the house, though a strongly built wooden one may be satisfactory. The lid should be covered with roofing felt to give extra protection.

For the storage of cleaning equipment, a good broom cupboard is essential. The most convenient type is at least 21 inches wide, and

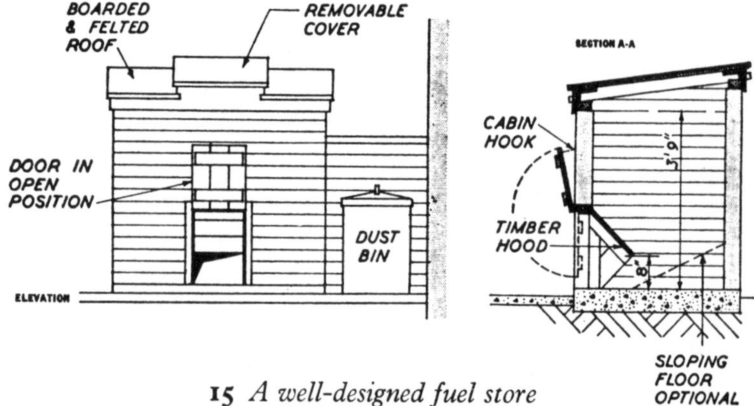

15 *A well-designed fuel store*

sufficiently deep to take a broom, carpet sweeper and suction cleaner; cleaning materials may be stored on a shelf in the upper part of the cupboard, and on small shelves fitted at the sides; short-handled brushes may be hung from hooks. According to the space available, the cupboard may be situated in the kitchen, utility room or hall.

Chapter 4

Floors and Floor Coverings

THERE IS NOW such a wide choice of flooring materials that considerable time and thought are often necessary when choosing them, and since most are expensive the selection is worth careful consideration, taking into account the various factors involved. To most people the appearance of the floor is of great importance; it is required to form a pleasing background to a particular scheme. Other properties, however, are closely linked; the appearance of the floor when it is new will soon be spoiled if it wears badly, or quickly soils and is not easily cleaned. Where traffic is likely to be heavy, durability is of primary importance; the floor must not scratch easily, nor show permanent dents from furniture. A floor which quickly becomes soiled is unsuitable for the living and working areas. The cause may lie in the colour, as in the case of white or very light tiles; or in the plainness of the material causing marks such as those from rubber heels to be conspicuous; or in the texture, which sometimes causes dirt to become embedded and difficult to remove. The warmth of the floor is a consideration in living-rooms, bedrooms and kitchens, especially in any room which is inadequately heated. A floor lacking in resilience, as everyone experiences at times, causes undue fatigue; a slippery floor is dangerous, particularly for old people and children, and causes strain which is tiring; a noisy floor may be a source of irritation and fatigue. It is difficult to find any floor which is excellent in every respect, and the weight given to the various factors will obviously depend upon the use of the room or area under consideration.

FLOORING MATERIALS

Wood

Wood is used in three ways: for a strip or board floor, made from softwood or hardwood 1–1½ inches thick; for a block floor, where the blocks of softwood or hardwood are 1–1½ inches thick, 6–15 inches long, and not more than 3½ inches wide; and for a parquet floor, where hardwoods ¼–¾ inch thick, chosen for their colour and beauty of graining, are laid on wooden sub-floors, and pinned and glued down. In appearance a wood floor is very attractive and various shades are possible; its wearing properties depend on the timber used. It is easily cleaned, and need not be slippery when suitable polish is used; it is reasonably warm and fairly quiet for most purposes. Wood is used also in combination with other materials; sawdust or wood chips are combined with synthetic resins and moulded under pressure.

Tiles

Clay tiles give a bare smooth floor which is very durable, easily cleaned, and suitable for heavy traffic purposes; unless highly polished they are not slippery. They are, however, poor with regard to warmth and resilience. They are available in a variety of qualities, colours and sizes, usually between 4 and 6 inches square. Concrete tiles up to 12 inches square are also available in various finishes. Thermoplastic tiles, made from various fillers and minerals bound together with synthetic resins, are made in a wide range of sizes and designs. These are much less cold and noisy than clay or concrete tiles; they are easily maintained if recommended methods are used, and are not slippery; they are durable, though unsuitable for very damp areas.

Polyvinyl Chloride

This, when used with various fillers, produces a flooring material in sheet or tile form which is hard wearing, easily cleaned, warm and quiet.

Terrazzo

This is a mixture of concrete and marble, which gives excellent wear, but is noisy and cold. If polished, it may become slippery.

Composition Floorings

Magnesite composition flooring is composed of various fillers and pigments combined with a solution of magnesium chloride; its hardness may be varied by the type and amount of fillers used. It is made in various colours, and gives very good wear, is not slippery, but is rather noisy and only moderately warm. An asphalt floor, made from combining bituminous materials with various coarse grits, is available in dark colours, and has similar properties, though it is not quite so durable. Combinations of cement and rubber are used for other jointless floorings.

Rubber

Rubber flooring is procurable in sheet or tile form in various degrees of hardness and finishes. It gives a floor which is warm and quiet, wearing well under most conditions. When wet, it is inclined to be slippery.

Cork

Cork tiles are made by heating granulated cork bark under pressure; the cork contains resins which bind it together; the resulting tiles are in varying shades of brown which give a good appearance. These tiles are fairly easily maintained provided a suitable polish is used sparingly; apart from denting easily, the floor wears well, is very warm, quiet and not slippery; it is often used in hospital wards, public libraries and other buildings where these properties are essential. For composition, rubber and cork floors the water wax emulsion type of polish is usually the most suitable and the least slippery.

Linoleum

This widely used floor covering was patented by a chemist named Walton in 1861, the idea being presented to him by the thick rubbery skin which forms on the top of paint which has been exposed to the air. The first ingredient which is used in linoleum manufacture is linseed oil, which is obtained from the seed of flax. The oil is pumped in films, in a heated building, on to layers of cotton scrim, and oxidised; the films are built up by degrees until the layer of oxidised oil approaches 1 inch in thickness, this process taking some months. The oxidised oil is then finely ground together with resins from various pine trees, and the mixture melted down; after cooling, it solidifies into slabs of what is known as linoleum cement. The cement is then finely shredded, and mixed by machinery with finely ground cork, sawdust and colourings, until all the ingredients are completely incorporated in granular form. Patterns are built up by various methods, and the granules pass between heated rollers under pressure, and are consolidated into smooth sheets on canvas foundations. After some weeks of maturing, during which time the linoleum becomes harder and more resilient, it is trimmed, inspected and packed into rolls 6 feet wide.

Linoleum is obtainable in many different qualities, colours and patterns, the best being inlaid, where the pattern is taken right through the thickness of the linoleum and will not therefore disappear in wear; cheap printed types wear badly and look shabby quickly, and should be avoided. Linoleum forms a hygienic, easily cleaned floor covering, and in soft plain colours provides an excellent background for other furnishings. Owing to its comparative coldness, it is, in living-rooms, most often used with rugs or as a surround to a carpet. In kitchens, a good quality linoleum is one of the most satisfactory floor coverings, and continues to hold its own in spite of the many more modern materials now available; the marbled or jaspé designs show marks less than a plain colour, and are preferable for use in a kitchen. Cork linoleum has a larger proportion of cork in its composition and is therefore less cold than ordinary linoleum.

Carpets

There is little doubt that the floor covering which has the widest appeal is the carpet. A carpet gives to a room that appearance of luxury which most people seek; it is both warm and comfortable; it can provide a pleasing, soft background to a colour scheme, or be the arresting focal point in it. If it is of good quality it will give excellent resistance to wear and last for many years; with modern equipment it is easily cleaned.

Traditional raw materials used for carpet weaving have been wool, jute and cotton, and traditional methods have resulted in the popular Axminster and Wilton carpets. Both varieties employ a backing of jute and cotton threads, and the pile is made of many thousand separate tufts of wool; these are anchored to the backing by different processes. In the manufacture of a Spool Axminster carpet, the tufts are secured to the warp threads by machinery, and cut, while the backing is in process of being woven. For the Chenille Axminster, two looms are used, one to bind the tufts together into a long length, the Chenille "fur", and the second to weave this into the fabric, in which it forms the weft. In making a Wilton carpet the wool is inserted in loops; these are raised to a standard height by a wire which is later withdrawn and cuts them; the best Wiltons are made of worsted yarns, and have strands woven into the back of the carpet, which reinforce it and make it exceptionally thick. Both Axminster and Wilton carpets are made in various qualities, the best having the greatest number of wool tufts to the inch. Both give very good wear and are very resilient, the thickness of the Wilton making it suitable especially where traffic is heavy. Both types continue to be the most popular, in spite of the advent of new methods and materials; the names Axminster and Wilton denote reliability, and these carpets have been tested over many years.

An uncut pile carpet, such as a Brussels or tapestry, is made similarly to the Wilton, and is less expensive but much less luxurious. Haircord carpeting is now produced in a wide range of qualities and attractive colourings; being very hard wearing, it is popular for stairs and dining-rooms, and anywhere calling for hard wear rather than luxurious softness.

More recent are the Needleloom and Tufted carpets, where, instead of the traditional methods of manufacture, the tufts are bonded to the base with rubber or with plastic composition, giving closeness which

16 *A double bedroom with single beds*

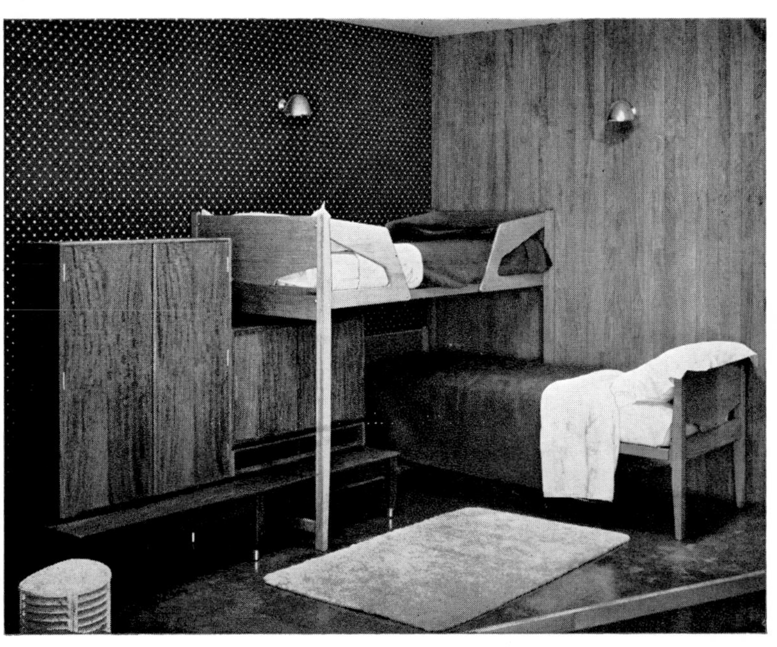

17 *A bedroom with bunks, suitable for two boys*

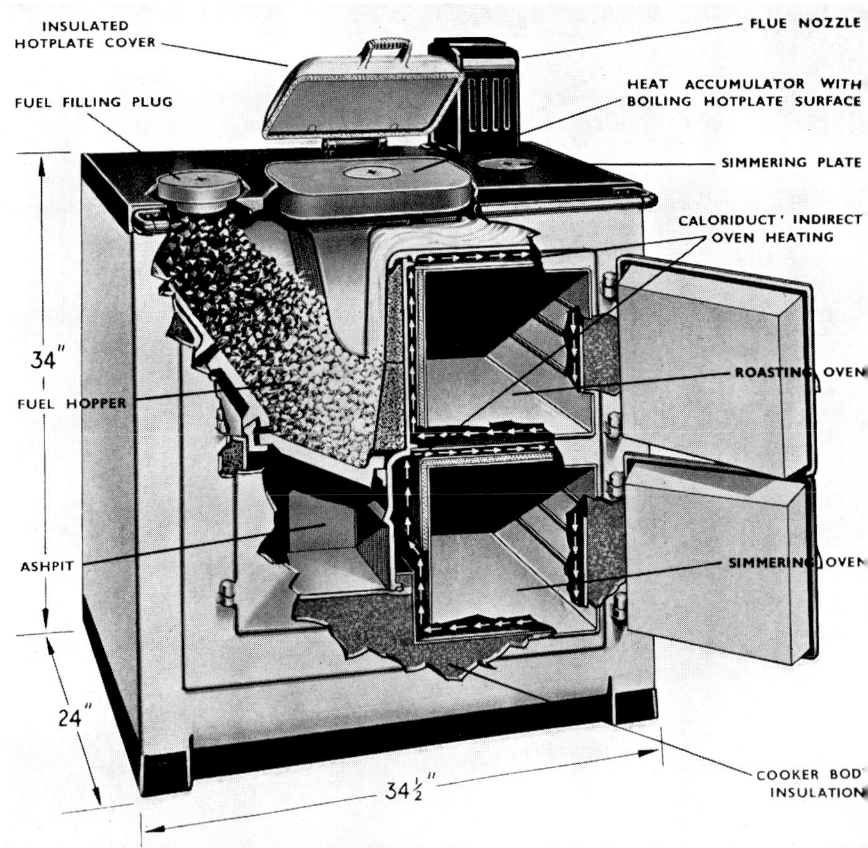

18 *A modern heat-storage cooker*

produces a strong and draught-proof floor covering. The method of manufacture prevents these carpets from fraying; they may easily be fitted by an amateur, requiring no binding, and this has increased their popularity; they cost less than a woven carpet.

The wool which forms the pile of a carpet is blended for hard wear and dyed by modern scientific methods which produce a wide range of beautiful colours; during dyeing, it can be treated with a moth-proofing agent which prolongs the life of the carpet. The pile is, however, no longer necessarily composed of wool, for the man-made fibres are now being used fairly widely; these have the advantage of being moth-proof, and are available in particularly soft, attractive shades; some lack the resilience of wool, tend to attract fluff and are at the same time less easily cleaned than a woollen carpet. Where the pile is made of rayon, reinforcing it with nylon does much to improve its strength.

In choosing a carpet, consideration should be given to the amount of traffic it will receive, and to the character and existing colour scheme of the room. A plain carpet always makes a pleasing background to a formal type of room, but the carpet which has several tones of one colour often gives interest in design and texture, and small marks are less noticeable, while the carpet with a more definite pattern is often preferred where wear is greatest. Where a carpet is fitted to cover an entire room, an appearance of space and luxury is achieved, and as there is no surround, the cleaning is simplified. For fitting wall to wall, carpeting strips are made in 27-inch and 36-inch widths; the use of broadloom seamless carpeting, obtainable in several wider widths, enables the room to be carpeted with few seams, and by using one of the easily applied adhesives, an amateur can fit the carpet successfully. The disadvantage of the fitted carpet is that, as it cannot be turned round, wear is likely to be uneven; moving the furniture occasionally into different positions helps to prevent this.

All carpets should have good underlays of felt or foam rubber. Floor boards often cause unsightly ridges along the carpet from dirt rising up from the space beneath, and sheets of newspaper or thick brown paper should be laid underneath the underlay to prevent this. A new carpet should be given about a month to settle before being cleaned with a suction cleaner, for all new carpets tend to shed loose pile. Grit should not be allowed to work into the back of the carpet, but suction cleaning is not usually advisable more frequently than once or twice a week.

In laying a stair carpet, an extra length of 1½–2 feet should be allowed so that the carpet may be moved up or down occasionally to even the wear. Stairs should be provided with strip underlay of felt or rubber, or pads, of the width of the carpet, and should overhang the edge of each step and be securely fixed. The pile of the carpet should run *down* the stairs.

Carpets which are not moth-proof should be protected yearly by spraying with an insecticide, particularly under heavy furniture and beneath the edges of the carpet and of the underlay. Stains should always be removed from a carpet as soon as possible.

Chapter 5

Space Heating

SOLID FUEL

Various ways of heating dwelling houses become popular in different climates. In Britain the open coal fire, in spite of its many drawbacks, has continued to hold its own. The labour caused by lifting and carrying coals, and in clearing ashes, is considerable. The fire is very often temperamental, difficult to light, smoky in certain winds; the interior decorations become dirty, and curtains and loose covers need frequent laundering. When the fire is first lit, the room temperature actually drops; the air which the fire requires for burning is drawn across the room from the doors and windows, and the draughts which occur are renewed each time fresh coal is added. Often the only part of the room to be really warm is a small area around the hearth. Yet there is something cheerful and companionable about an open fire which people are loath to abolish; as a focal point to a room it provides a much friendlier atmosphere than the television set, and one more conducive to conversation.

The old type of fire with high bars and uncontrolled draught was only 18 per cent efficient. By efficiency is meant the amount of heat actually given out into the room compared with the total amount produced by the fuel; by modern methods it is possible to measure this, and careful and accurate estimates can be made. A fire which burns 1 pound of coal in 1 hour produces in that time 12,000 British Thermal Units of heat; if the heat given to the room is found by measurement to be 3000 British Thermal Units, 25 per cent of the total, this fire is said to have an efficiency of 25 per cent.

Coal is a mineral substance of which there are still good, though not unlimited, supplies in the country, and as the coal pits of necessity become deeper, it is more difficult and more expensive to obtain it. Although coal is very inflammable, its combustion in the old type of fireplace was incomplete and produced much smoke. Smoke consists of various gases, including hydrogen and sulphur, and solid carbon in a fine state of division, which do much damage when sent into the air. Thousands of tons of soot are deposited annually; damage is done to crops; the smoky atmosphere, by excluding ultra-violet rays, has a bad effect on health; it has a bad psychological effect; buildings become dirty and decay. It is therefore essential that coal should be used more efficiently and more economically than in the past, and much research has gone into the improvement of the various appliances which burn it. Most of these burn the small sizes of coal produced by modern mining; these smaller coals expose a large surface to the air, and, provided that the air supply is adequate, burn well and more economically than the larger lumps which used to be preferred because they helped the old wasteful fires to burn more slowly. The coal is nowadays graded into sizes at the pithead; it is then freed from stone and shale by hand cleaning; for small sizes, the "dirt" is removed in water, or by vibrating the coals in currents of air.

The problem of smoke may be overcome by burning not the crude coal which produces the smoke, but one which is virtually smokeless.

Anthracite is a small, hard, shiny, natural coal with a high carbon content. It is difficult to ignite, but burns slowly, producing very little smoke. Its main uses are for stoves, boilers and cookers.

Welsh dry steam coal is another natural smokeless fuel, fairly similar in appearance to anthracite, and used largely for boilers and as a foundation for processed fuels.

Coke is produced in various forms. In the manufacture of gas coke, coal is heated in retorts to 1000° Centigrade for 10 to 12 hours. The volatile products are driven off and recovered as gas, and its valuable by-products and coke are left.

For the production of hard coke, the coal is heated to 1300°C. for 24 hours. Some hard coke is valuable for domestic purposes, but most is used in industry. Low temperature coke is produced by heating selected coals to about 650°C. The resulting coke is sold under various trade names; it is very light in weight, has more volatile matter than ordinary coke and is more easily ignited.

Carbonised ovoids are made by heating ground Welsh dry steam coal mixed with pitch and moulded into ovoid shape; volatile constituents are driven off by further heating, and the resulting fuel is sold under the trade name of Phurnacite. Other ovoids and brickettes are made from coal dust mixed with pitch and pressed into shape; these are smoky, and useful for open fires only.

Before examining the improvements in the design of appliances burning solid fuel, it is necessary to understand how heat is transferred from them into a room. The open coal fire of the type to which people have become accustomed sends out its heat by radiation; this means that it strikes objects in the room without heating the air in between. It is possible, when standing in front of a recently lit fire, to feel the rays of heat, even though the air in the room is still cold. In time, the objects heated begin to warm the air immediately around them, but the fire itself heats by radiation only. When, however, some form of convection heating is employed by the fire, the air in the room is heated and rises, cold air falls and takes its place, and this circulation continues until in time all the air in the room becomes very warm, and adequate ventilation is essential to prevent the room from becoming overheated. Appliances give their heat by radiation, or by convection, or are designed to utilise both methods.

A simple modern grate may be fitted to an existing open fireplace

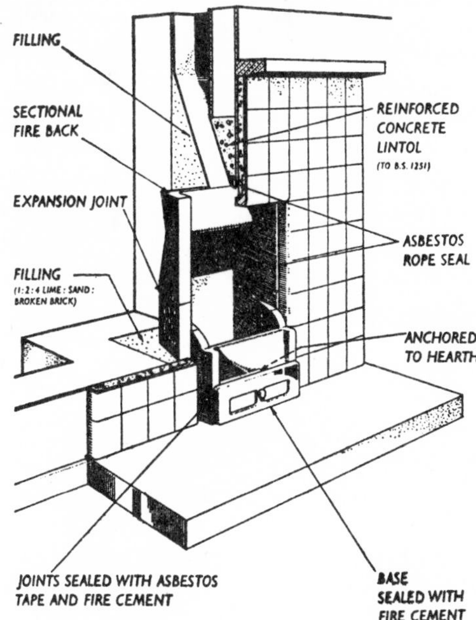

19 *A modern open fire*

with very little expense, and with considerable advantage. The continuously burning fire may be kept in overnight with little trouble; this maintains an even temperature and provides a comfortable room for cold winter mornings, is especially useful where there are elderly people, but is also a convenience and comfort for a housewife. The vitreous enamel of which the modern fires are made is available in a variety of colours to suit different schemes, and is easily cleaned with a damp cloth. The fires are designed to burn several different fuels, but are particularly suitable for smokeless fuels; they have efficient draught control which can be adjusted according to the type of fuel in use and the rate of burning required. Removable ash-pans simplify the clearing out of the grate, though in some designs these are not sufficiently large, with the result that a considerable amount of ash falls behind and to the sides of the ash-pan. Many of these fires are higher than the older types, though some have a front panel which drops to reveal more of the fire and to radiate at a low level. Back boilers may be fitted; gas ignition is another additional fixture and is a great advantage.

More expensive, but certainly more efficient, is the convector open fire (Fig. 20), which may be either inset or free-standing. This has the advantages already described, but in addition air is drawn into a space

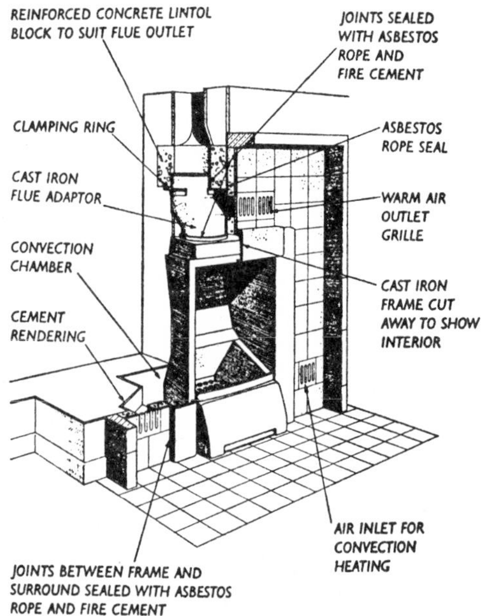

20 *A convector open fire*

behind the fire, is warmed, and returns to the room again through vents. The room is therefore heated by radiation and convection. Where it is fairly small and radiant heat is found to be sufficient, the convected heat may be taken through ducts to another room, where it provides what is known as background heating. This is not the equivalent of the convected heat of a central heating installation; it does, however, take the chill off the air, provide more comfortable conditions for a housewife working in different parts of the house, and prevent condensation and the subsequent risk of damp clothing. It is not advisable to attempt to warm more than one additional room from the one fire, and it should not be done at all unless convected heat is really not required in the room where the fire is situated. A convenient arrangement makes it possible to convey the warmed air either to this room or to another, according to what is required at the time. Another feature of many modern convector fires is the restricted chimney throat, which reduces the loss of warmed air up the flue.

A further improvement is the convector open fire which is made to draw the air it requires for burning through a duct running under the floor boards. This fire has a deep ash-pan which needs to be emptied once weekly. Draughts in the room are greatly lessened, since the air

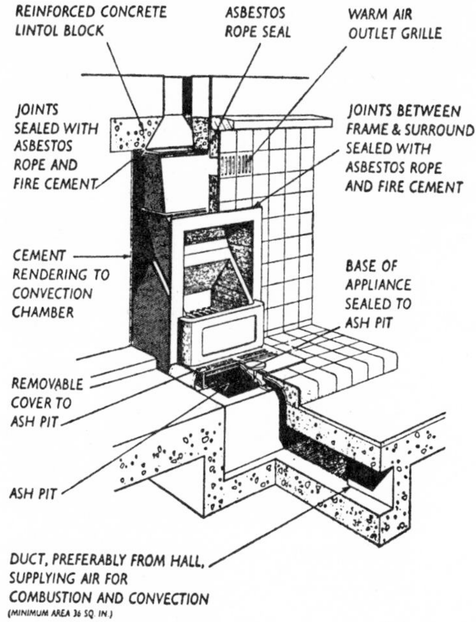

21 *A convector open fire with deep ash pit*

for combustion is not drawn across the floor, but underneath it. Only by completely sealing doors and windows, however, could draughts be wholly eliminated. This type of fire is most easily installed during the building of a new house, but may be put into an existing house except where a solid floor prevents under-hearth air supply (Fig. 21).

The most efficient and most economical heating device is the stove, traditionally used in Continental countries. In Britain it has been less popular because of its appearance, but its use is becoming more widespread than it used to be. Many modern stoves have doors which may be opened so that the fire is visible when required, and this has increased their popularity. Most are free-standing; they may be placed in front

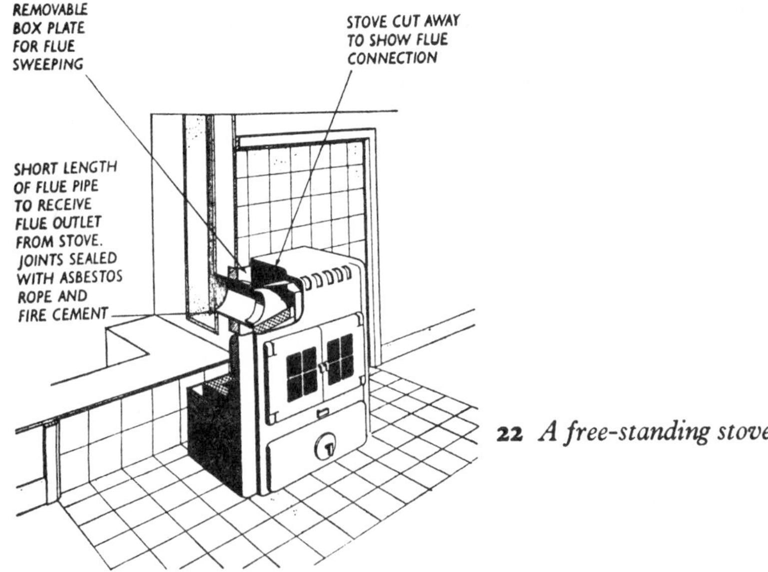

22 *A free-standing stove*

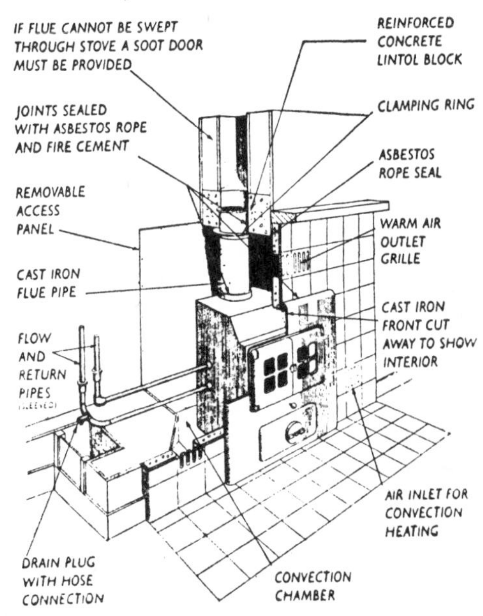

23 *An inset stove*

of an existing fireplace. Others are inset like a convector fire, with grilles in the casing through which warm air is emitted; the amount of radiation is less than from a convector fire. In the closed stoves, the heating is mainly by convection, and the whole room is kept evenly warm; efficiency is high, and the stoves will heat at low running costs. Next in order of merit for efficiency are the openable stoves.

In all modern fires and stoves the draught control is so efficient that a very low fire may be quickly boosted; with a stove, if by mistake the draught control is left open for any length of time, there is danger of the chimney catching fire. Whatever type of modern fire is selected, the recommended fuels and sizes of fuel should be ascertained and used; almost all the fires are suitable for a wide range of fuels, so there is seldom much difficulty in obtaining supplies.

ELECTRICITY

The electric appliance which is most commonly used for space heating is probably the electric fire. In a house where the main type of heating used is by solid fuel, there are many times in the spring and summer when, even though the days are warm enough to do without it, the evenings are so cool that some form of heating becomes essential for comfort, and then the electric fire is particularly useful. In houses where there is no central or background heating, electric fires provide comfort for undressing in cold bedrooms, or for meals rooms or alcoves. Even where there is adequate central heating in a living-room, an electric fire is often used in addition, to give cheerfulness and provide a focal point. The convenience and cleanliness of this form of heating make it very popular; it is completely labour-saving, it is obtainable in a variety of designs, and it requires no flue, being either portable, when only a plug socket is necessary, or inset in whatever area of the room most requires it.

There are two main types of electric fire. The first is the fire-bar type, with coiled wire, wound in grooves in fireclay, which becomes red hot and heats the fireclay; this emits about 50 per cent of its heat by radiation from the front of the fire, the remainder heating the framework of the fire, which in turn warms the air around and behind it, setting up convection currents. This type is very useful when the warming of the whole room, for some hours at a time, is required.

The second is the reflector type, where the heating element is fitted to a polished metal reflector which sends out a concentrated beam of radiant heat; the reflector may be circular, parabolic or trough shaped. The reflector itself remains comparatively cool, as owing to its shiny surface it does not absorb heat, and the full heat is felt within a very few minutes. As a rule, this type gives out more of its heat by radiation than the fire-bar type; it is very suitable for intermittent use, or at meal times. As in the case of a solid fuel fire heating by radiation, in time the warmed objects in the room heat the air around them, and convection takes place; the time taken for all the air in a room to become warm will, however, be longer than with a fire designed to heat partly by convection.

Other types of electric appliance heat by convection only. Tubular heaters are available in various lengths, and may be fitted around the skirting board, either singly or in rows of two or three. The tubes are heated to a surface temperature of about 180°F. (82°C.) in under 15

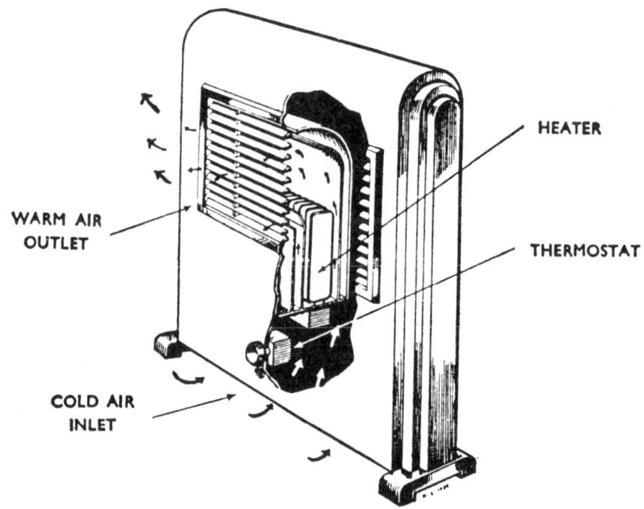

24 *An electric convector heater*

minutes, and because of the length of heating area, the warmed air is well distributed over the room. When the tubular heater is placed beneath a window, any incoming cold air is warmed, and draughts are avoided. In cloakrooms, where some form of heating is required at times to dry damp clothing, these heaters are useful.

Another type of electric convector heater is in the form of a cabinet with an electric element inside it, an inlet for cold air at the bottom, and an outlet for warm air at the top (Fig. 24). Heating-up is rapid; the amount of heat given varies according to the size and type of heater, and many are thermostatically controlled. The heaters are portable; when placed beneath a window they check draughts; when they are placed in a hall, the warmed air circulates through the house, and makes a considerable difference to its comfort. Electric fans are fitted to some models in order to speed up the circulation of warm air.

An electric radiator filled with water is similar to one which forms part of a central heating system, but here the radiator itself has an electric heating element. Owing to the amount of water to be heated, this takes some little time, but the heat is retained after the current has been turned off. A steam-filled radiator, with a smaller quantity of water involved, is also available. The electric radiator which is oil filled has largely superseded the water and steam varieties. The surface does not reach a dangerously high temperature, and is thermostatically controlled; it takes about 20 minutes to reach its full heat (and to cool); since nothing is lost by evaporation, no topping-up is necessary, and there is no risk of damage by frost. It should be noted that although termed "radiators", all these appliances are more correctly called convectors, since most of their heat is emitted in this way, and only a small amount of low-temperature radiant heat is produced.

Electric panel heaters may be either portable, when they can be placed in cold parts of rooms to supplement other forms of heating, or fixed to the walls or ceiling, where they may be mounted or recessed. When mounted, the panels may be fitted into the decoration scheme; when recessed, they will not be visible. They are made of metal or glass and contain heating elements, and are backed by insulating material. The surface of the panel is raised to a temperature of about 300°F. (149°C.), and gives most of its heat to the room as low-temperature radiation. Another system of heating the fabric of the walls or ceiling is to incorporate electrically heated wires which raise the surface temperature to about 100°F. (40°C.).

Electric floor heating (Fig. 25) is a new development which is being used in new houses, offices and factories. The electric elements, made of special steel enclosed in thick polyvinyl chloride sheathing, are laid in ducts in a solid concrete floor. The elements can be withdrawn without disturbing the floor surface, but breakdowns are very rare, and the heating installation is said to last as long as the building itself. Most of the usual floor finishes, such as wood, tiles and thermoplastic tiles, and floor coverings such as carpet and linoleum, are suitable. The temperature of the floor reaches 75°F. (24°C.), and is controlled so as not to exceed this. Where the concrete floor is sufficiently thick, it is possible to use the electricity during the night only, at special low peak rates of charging; the heat stored is then given off during the day, and in a well-designed installation the lowering of temperature by the end of the day is unnoticeable. No maintenance is necessary. A portable type of electric floor warming is provided by a heater made to fit underneath a carpet. Elements sheathed in plastic are fixed in place between two layers of material, the covering material varying in type according to whether it is intended for use with or without an additional underlay. With some heaters, automatic switches and thermostatic control

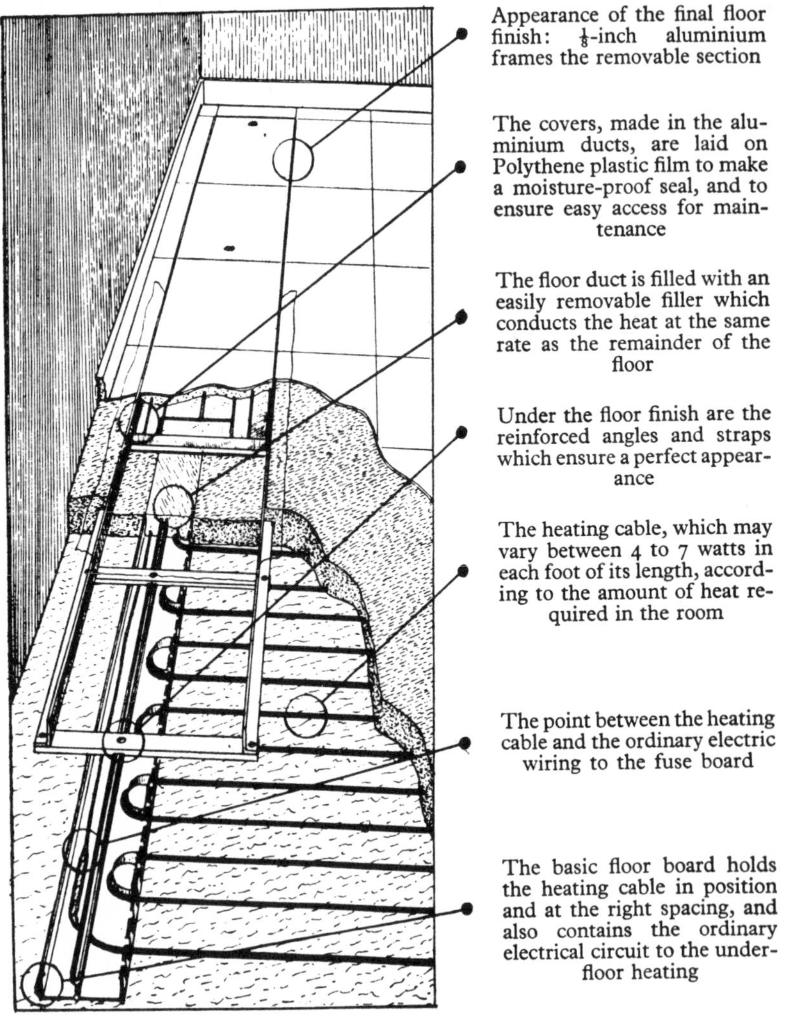

25 *Electric floor heating*

are provided. The heater must be switched on one to two hours before it is required, and provides a temperature of about 75°F. (24°C.) on the surface of the carpet.

A method of using electricity at the lowest possible cost is provided by the storage heater, at present used chiefly in commercial and industrial buildings. A metal block container is filled with a material such as concrete which will absorb and store heat; a heating element is fitted inside. As in the case of the thick concrete floor, heat is stored during the night and given out during the day.

Infra-red radiation is a new method of heating, where the element is sheathed in pure fused silica in the form of a tube, transparent and capable of withstanding the high temperature. The result is a safe type of heater, which may be fixed to the walls of bathrooms and kitchens without danger, or used outside for overhead shop window heating, and is said to be good from the point of view of health.

GAS

The most usual type of gas fire has a series of burners at the lower front of the fire; these heat fireclay radiants which send heat into the room, while the products of combustion pass up the chimney. These fires may be fixed to stand at the level of the hearth, or to be built in at that level, or to form a built-in panel higher than the hearth. Other fires are portable, and can be carried from room to room and plugged in as required; of these, the large portable fires must be used in a fireplace, so that the products of combustion will escape through the flue, while small types may be used at any point in the room; if these are to be in use for any length of time, adequate ventilation should be ensured. Small portable fires are fitted with chromium-plated reflectors. All modern gas fires are made with good design and attractive colourings to harmonise with existing decorations; the luminous or "neat" flames burn silently and economically, and the radiants now used are very hard wearing. Heat output is often controlled by economy taps giving three or four heating positions; many fires have been fitted with automatic ignition, so that the turning of the gas tap lights the burners, and taps are often placed at a convenient height to avoid the necessity of stooping.

A fire which is more efficient than the radiant type is one which heats by radiation and convection. Cold air is drawn in beneath, or in some models at points above and below, the burners, and is warmed as it passes round the sides and back, being emitted into the room through the convector grille at the top. As in the case of solid fuel fires, some convector gas fires have a device which restricts the chimney throat in order to prevent excessive up draught. These fires are intended to be used for long periods when it is desirable to warm the whole of a room efficiently and economically.

The background heating which is so particularly useful in halls, and gives warmth in some degree to the whole house, may be provided by various types of gas convector heaters. These may stand in well-ventilated areas without a flue; some are portable, others are fixed to the floor, and other small gas heaters are made to be fixed to the wall. A glow which is visible through the lower grilles of some heaters gives an additional impression of warmth and comfort; others, though primarily convectors, provide visible radiants as well.

OIL

So much advance has been made in the design of heating appliances where oil is used as a fuel that past disadvantages have practically disappeared. The modern oil heater is as neat in appearance as gas and electric heaters; it is light enough to carry from room to room, and is safe to leave without attention for long periods in between fillings if the maker's instructions are correctly followed; it is inexpensive to buy, economical to run, and burns without odour.

Oil heaters burn the fuel in one of two ways. In the first, a reservoir for oil is situated at the bottom of the heater; a wick is fitted which becomes soaked with oil; this is held in position by a burner, and is raised or lowered as required by turning a regulating knob; the wick is lit, and when it is adjusted to the correct height a blue flame is produced which burns without smoking and gives intense heat. In the second type, the fuel burnt is paraffin vapour; this is pumped to the burner and, when alight, heats an element. This pressure method is used in some of the smaller oil heaters which heat by radiation; the fire is fitted with a plated reflector, and resembles an electric or gas bowl fire. It has particular advantage where quick results in heating are required.

Convector oil heaters are designed to be very similar in appearance to any other modern types, with openings at the bottom for the entry of cold air, and at the top where the warmed air is emitted. In some, a fitted reflecting plate gives a warm cheerful glow. Another type is the oil burning "radiator", resembling a central heating radiator, but portable; this provides good background heating.

CENTRAL HEATING

By this is meant the warming of some or all of the rooms of a house, by either hot water or hot air from one boiler fired by any of the fuels in use. Temperatures which are considered desirable for comfort are, for the living-room, 65°–70°F. (18°–21°C.), for bedrooms, hall and landing, 55°F. (12°–13°C.), and for the bathroom, 60°F. (15°–16°C.).

Hot Water

In large buildings, the central heating system is separate from the domestic hot water system, and two boilers are therefore required.

In a small house, especially where an open fire is used, partial central heating may be sufficient for comfort. This may be provided by a large back boiler heated by an open fire or by a modern thermostatically controlled independent boiler, both supplying enough hot water for domestic use and several radiators. Full central heating is supplied by a sectional boiler, with a rated output of 33,000 B.T.U.s per hour and upwards according to size, or by the modern gravity feed boiler, in which the fuel is fed automatically from a hopper to the small intense fire, to which air may be supplied by a thermostatically controlled electric fan. Instead of ash removal a clinker is removed daily. The rated output is 35,000 B.T.U.s per hour and upwards.

A modern development has been that of small bore central heating. For this, ½- or ⅜-in. pipes are used instead of 1- to 2-in. ones, and the water is forced through these by a small economical electric pump. The pipes, being inconspicuous, may be taken through the house with little disturbance to its structure.

Wherever one boiler is used for both domestic hot water and central heating, an indirect cylinder is essential. Water from the boiler passes through a coil or inner cylinder inside the hot water storage cylinder, and returns to the boiler; radiators for central heating are connected to this primary circuit, in which the same water circulates continuously. Evaporation losses are made good from a cold water tank, but, apart from this, no fresh water enters to cool the system; furring of boiler, pipes and radiators by hard water, or rusting by soft water, is also avoided. Water for domestic use is heated indirectly by the coil in the cylinder and circulates to the taps, but does not itself pass through the boiler.

Radiators are constructed to give a large heating surface, the air surrounding which is warmed and rises by convection, and since this causes dust and dirt to be deposited on the wall surface above, radiators are usually placed beneath windows, which has the added advantage of causing the incoming cold air to be warmed. Wall radiators made in standard panels are neat and easy to keep clean, while the skirting radiator, a recent development, is inconspicuous and distributes its heat evenly.

Hot Air

The simplest method of heating a house by warm air, a modified form of central heating, is based on the Roman hypocaust; air, warmed by a furnace in the basement, rises by convection through a grating in the floor above the furnace and circulates through the house. An improved method causes the warmed air to pass through ducts to the rooms in the house, and back to the furnace room to be reheated and circulated.

A further improvement is the provision of an electric fan at the side of the heating chamber, which blows the warm air along the ducts. Where fresh air from outside can be introduced into the system, the method becomes more expensive as more fuel is used.

Warm air heating has been popular in America for some years; in Britain it is now rapidly developing. The heating unit burns gas, oil or a smokeless solid fuel; heaters differ in size and design, but follow the same principle; air enters the unit, and is warmed by passing over a heat exchanger; it is then fanned through ducts to the various rooms in the house. The system is controlled by a thermostat placed in the living-room or hall; when the required temperature is reached, the supply of fuel, or rate of burning, is controlled, and the fan switched off. The warm air supply may be shut off from any room, if required, by closing the grille. Some units are designed to heat both air and the domestic hot water, the storage cylinder standing within the unit, and the water being heated by contact with the hot air and by radiant heat from the furnace.

With the larger heating units, full warming is supplied to the whole house, while smaller models supply full heating to the living-room and background heating to the bedrooms. The system is inconspicuous, as the ducts are hidden in the walls or beneath floors, outlet grilles are often in ceilings, and the heating units built into cupboards or recesses. Ideally, the system should be installed during the building of a house; it may, however, be installed in existing houses, though this entails structural alterations.

Whichever form of central heating is employed has both advantages and disadvantages. It provides a constant and easily controlled temperature throughout the whole house, and to those accustomed to the draughty halls and chilly bedrooms in houses without it, this seems very desirable; the system is labour-saving, since an efficient boiler needs little attention, and no carrying of fuel or clearing of ashes from the warmed rooms is entailed. There is, however, the tendency for the air to become overheated and dry, with consequent stuffiness and discomfort; good ventilation is essential. Whether the lack of an open fire, with its cheerfulness and companionship, is or is not a serious disadvantage is a debatable point; many people cease to miss it when they have become used to central heating.

DISTRICT HEATING

Both in America and in several European countries it is the custom to supply heating for groups of houses and blocks of flats from a central source, such as the boiler of a power station. This very large boiler has a higher degree of efficiency than the smaller domestic variety can attain, and the method, when used on a large scale, is found to be satisfactory. District heating is now in use in several areas of Great Britain, both for housing estates and flats. In some cases, the steam from the central boiler is used to heat the water for central heating and domestic use; in others, the heated water is conveyed directly from the boiler to the houses or flats. The temperature can be controlled by individual tenants.

VENTILATION

By ventilation is meant the process of changing air and, by doing so, ridding the room of products of combustion and respiration, together with bacteria, tobacco smoke and odours of perspiration and cooking. It is of particular importance where flueless gas appliances are in use; where any infection is present, small particles are apt to accumulate where ventilation is insufficient; where odour of perspiration is perceptible, it should be taken as a sign that ventilation is inadequate.

The temperature of the body remains nearly constant; in good conditions, the loss of heat from it is sufficient to balance the amount produced. The body loses heat by evaporation, respiration, convection and radiation to its surroundings and by conduction through clothing. This heat loss must be understood in considering the discomfort experienced from remaining in a crowded and badly ventilated place for any length of time.

In extreme cases, such as the packed train carriage with tightly closed windows, discomfort may be due to an unduly high concentration of carbon dioxide from respiration, and a lowering of oxygen. In a normal room, the changes in oxygen and carbon dioxide will probably be too small for ill effects, and the discomfort will arise from other causes. When the room is crowded with people, and there is no adequate ventilation, the air in it becomes hot and loaded with moisture. At this stage, further evaporation from the skin becomes impossible; as the temperature of the room rises, heat loss by radiation and convection from the body is lowered; the sole remaining way to rid the body of heat is by respiration. While a limited time of exposure to such conditions will cause yawning, headache and possible faintness, the constant exposure imposed by working daily in badly ventilated rooms may lead to a lowering of general health and a predisposition to respiratory diseases such as colds, catarrh and bronchitis. It is found that part of the discomfort experienced from bad ventilation is somewhat decreased if the air is set in motion.

Natural ventilation is achieved when currents of fresh air are brought

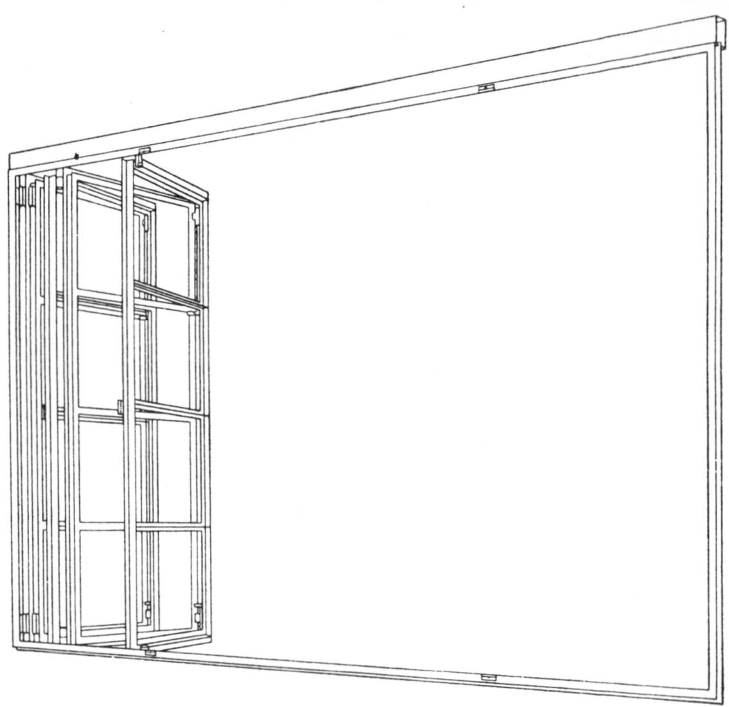

26 *Sliding windows*

into a room; as it becomes heated by contact with the people in the room, and with walls and objects, convection currents are set up. The best ventilation is produced from windows at opposite sides of the room so that cross currents are set in motion. The sash window usual in older types of houses ensured good ventilation when it was opened at the top and at the bottom, though in cold weather this was sometimes uncomfortable, and only half the window area could be open at any time. The tendency in building modern homes is to ensure the maximum amount of sunlight and fresh air by providing large window spaces of the casement type, often at both ends of a room, so that good ventilation can easily be obtained without draughts; where central heating is also installed, it is particularly important to ventilate well. Schoolrooms and public buildings are usually ventilated by horizontally or vertically pivoted windows; these swing on a central axis, so that when fully open, half the window swings into the room and the other half swings outside. Hopper ventilators are often fitted in addition; these are about 18 inches high, and are hinged to open backwards into the room, with side cheeks of steel or glass to prevent draughts. Modern schools often have very wide windows running the entire length of the classrooms, opening by means of hinged sections which fold back upon one another; these slide on metal tracks, and the space can be partially or fully opened.

In large public buildings such as theatres, concert halls and factories,

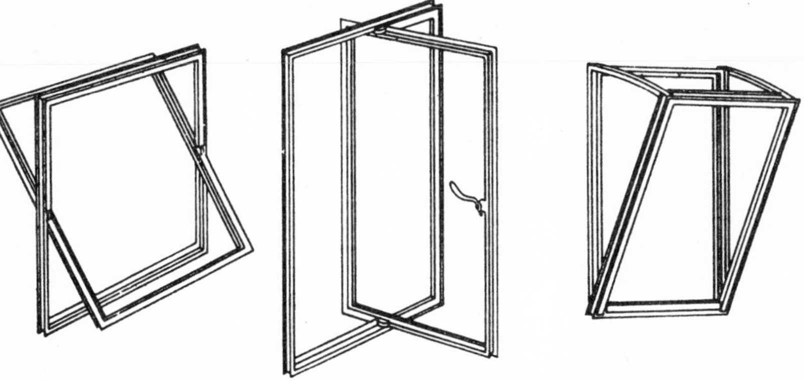

27 *Windows: horizontally pivoted; vertically pivoted; hopper ventilator with glass sides*

natural ventilation is not always possible and artificial or mechanical ventilation has to be employed. Here fresh air entering the building is conveyed through ducts to the various outlet points, while powerful fans are used to extract the used air. The system is combined with heating in the winter months.

Chapter 6

Water Heating, Cooking and Lighting

HOT WATER SUPPLY

For reasons of personal and domestic hygiene, and to ensure the smooth running of the house without unnecessary labour and irritation, a really efficient method of water heating is one of the most essential features of a comfortable home. The circulation of the water has been considered; the choice of a method of heating it is dependent on the installation costs, running costs, storage space available for fuel, space for fitting the heating appliance and ease of operation. For the majority of households, the stored hot water supply is usually found to be most satisfactory, though other methods prove very suitable for some circumstances.

Independent Boilers

The modern boiler, made to fit well into the modern kitchen, is pleasant in appearance and finished in vitreous enamel; it burns a variety of fuels, of which the smokeless ones are to be preferred. It has a high thermal efficiency; in the most labour-saving boilers, this is achieved by the air supply to the fire being thermostatically controlled so that no dampers are required. The amount of hot water available will depend on the size of the boiler, the size of the storage cylinder, good arrangement of service pipes, and efficient lagging of pipes and cylinder; but even with small boilers, it is possible to heat a towel rail which gives warmth to the bathroom, and, with larger boilers, some radiators, so that partial central heating is obtained in addition to the domestic hot water, while the boiler itself provides comfortable warmth in the kitchen. With most appliances, stoking is necessary not more than twice, and possibly only once, in 24 hours, and is simplified by improvements in the placing and design of refuelling holes; in some appliances, the gravity feed arrangement simplifies it still further by supplying fuel to the fire automatically, as it becomes necessary. The riddling of the boiler fire, and the clearing away of ash, has in the past caused inevitable dust in the kitchen; this disadvantage has been overcome by the provision of well-designed ash-pans into which all the ash is directed, and screening devices to prevent any ash escaping during riddling; with some big boilers, the removal of a clinker is the only labour involved daily. Provided that a good smokeless fuel is used, modern boilers will remain burning for months without requiring to be let out, and cleaning of flues is necessary only occasionally.

Many of the solid fuel boilers are available also for oil burning, and this has many advantages. Oil is a comparatively cheap fuel, especially when purchased in bulk; it is delivered by an oil company as required, usually with very little delay, and supplied to a tank which must be placed outside the house above the level of the boiler, so that it will feed it by gravity. The flow of oil to the burner is controlled by a thermostat, according to the temperature of water required, and running costs are low. The arrangement for storage adds to the initial cost of installation, but the system is completely labour-saving, and extremely efficient; there is no carrying of fuel, stoking and clearing of ash, and the boiler will operate for months without attention. The cleaning of the burner is a simple operation, and necessary only occasionally. An existing boiler designed for burning solid fuel may be fitted with a conversion unit for burning oil, the cost varying according to the size of the boiler and storage tank for oil. For converting a small boiler used for domestic hot water supply only, it is possible to cut the initial cost by omitting the large outside storage tank, and using instead of it a small tank to stand beside the boiler.

Boilers Heated by Open Fires and Solid Fuel Cookers

The addition of a boiler behind an open fire adds to its efficiency by utilising more of its heat; since the fire is then serving two purposes, it is an economical method of water heating. The fact that it is not possible to heat water without heating the room is a disadvantage in very warm weather, and for this reason it is worth while providing an alternative method of water heating for the summer months. If the back boiler is to work efficiently, the position of the fire must be considered in relation to the points where hot water will be drawn off, and unnecessary lengths of piping avoided; both pipes and storage cylinder should be lagged.

Most of the modern solid fuel cookers incorporate boilers and, provided they are sensibly managed, will provide an adequate supply of hot water. With the smaller type of cooker, it is not usually possible to draw the heat to the oven and have large quantities of hot water at the same time; this is not a serious disadvantage, since the bulk of hot water is required after cooking is finished, and it is unusual to plan much baking for a wash-day.

Where a solid fuel boiler, either independent or heated by an open fire, is the water-heating medium for the winter months, it is useful to install an alternative method for the summer, and this can be achieved in various ways by using either gas or electricity. Any of these methods may, of course, be chosen for water heating all the year round, in preference to solid fuel, being labour-saving, useful for small flats, for families out most of the day, and where it is unnecessary to provide warmth for the kitchen from a boiler fire.

Gas

The gas circulator (Fig. 28) is a small container for water fitted below the hot water storage cylinder, and connected with it by two pipes—flow and return. The water in the circulator is heated by a gas jet, and rises up the flow pipe, which conveys it to the top of the cylinder, while cold water from the bottom of the cylinder flows in to take its place, through the return pipe, entering the circulator at the bottom, and passing over a thermostat. As soon as the cylinder is full of hot water, this returning water will become hot, and will bring the thermostat into operation, reducing the size of the gas flame. When any water is drawn off, and the cylinder is replenished from the cold tank, the water returning to the circulator will be cold again, and the gas burner will come on fully. With these and other methods used as alternatives to solid fuel, the water in the solid fuel boiler will not circulate when the boiler fire is out, being at a lower level. When the boiler is in use, it is possible to use the circulator to boost the hot water, though with a modern boiler and good insulation this should not be necessary.

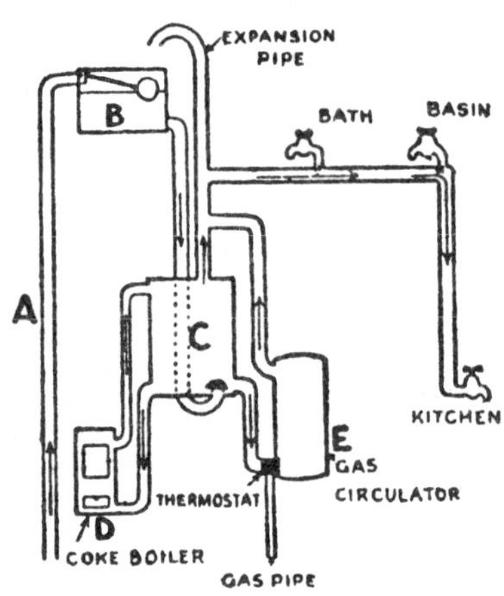

28 *Diagram of a gas circulator:* A, *cold water pipe feeding cistern* B; C, *hot water storage tank;* D, *coke boiler;* E, *gas circulator*

The gas storage heater is a self-contained water heater working on the same principle as the circulator. The circulator is inside a well-lagged storage container, and is thermostatically controlled. The capacities of these heaters vary according to requirements; small heaters are obtainable for sink purposes only, larger ones for baths. When the total quantity is required at one time, some delay takes place while further supplies are being heated.

In the instantaneous gas heater (Fig. 29), the water is heated as it flows through it, so that it is made available very quickly. The gas is turned on, and a small pilot flame is lit. When the hot tap is turned on, cold water enters the heater, and passes through a restrictor (venturi tube); by the pressure of the water, an automatic gas valve is opened to allow gas to reach the burners; the burners are lit by the pilot flame, and flare up, heating the water as it passes through a heat exchanger, and continuing to do so for as long as the tap remains open. Small

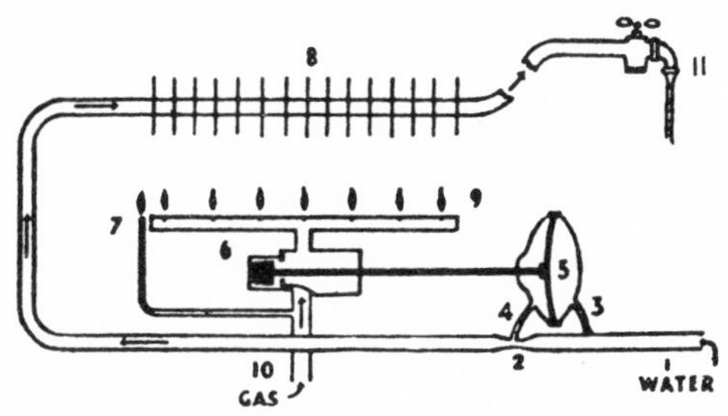

29 *Diagram of an instantaneous gas water heater:* 1, *water;* 2, *venturi tube;* 3 *and* 4, *pipes;* 5, *diaphragm;* 6, *valve;* 7, *pilot flame;* 8, *heat exchanger;* 9, *burners;* 10, *gas pipe;* 11, *hot water tap*

geysers are available for use at one sink only, larger ones may be fitted for supplying baths, and multi-point heaters are connected to several taps. It is also possible to have a multi-point heater fitted to an existing hot water system, and used as an alternative to solid fuel; in this case, by an arrangement of valves, the water in the storage tank may be put out of circulation, so that it will be unaffected by the flow of water through the geyser.

Electricity

The electric immersion heater is probably the most commonly used appliance for water heating as an alternative to a solid fuel system. The heater is fitted inside the existing cylinder; it is completely immersed in the water, and therefore no wastage of heat is possible at that point. It should be placed at a low level in the cylinder, since it heats the water in its immediate vicinity, which begins to rise to the top of the cylinder, and is displaced by cooler, heavier water. Most immersion heaters are now thermostatically controlled. Where an immersion heater is installed, it is of great importance to lag the cylinder and the service pipes thoroughly; a loss of 86 units per week from an unlagged, 30-gallon cylinder, where the water is heated to 140°F. (60°C.), may be reduced to seven units by lagging the cylinder with a 3-inch thickness of granulated cork.

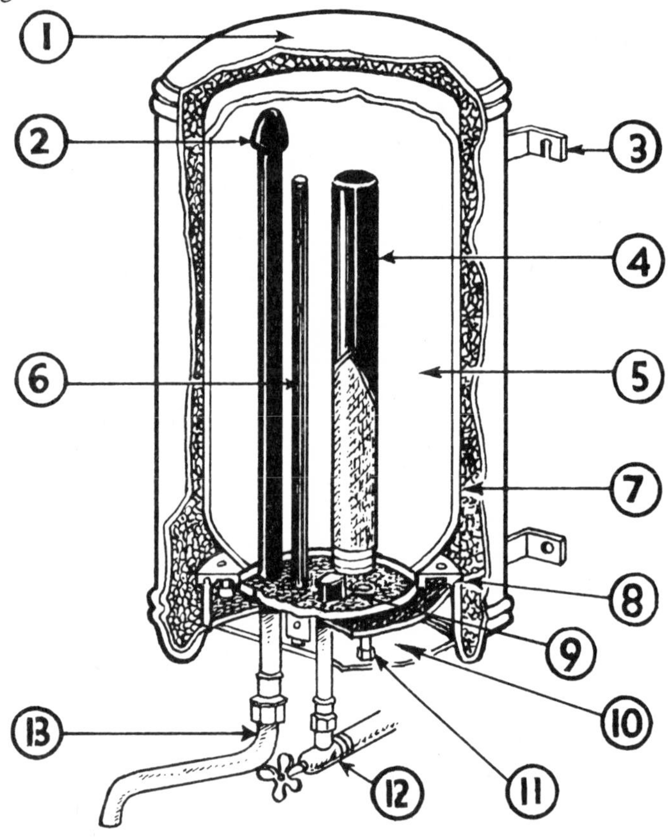

30 *Electric storage heater:* 1, *outer case;* 2, *anti-drip syphon;* 3, *wall-fixing bracket;* 4, *element;* 5, *tinned copper water chamber;* 6, *thermostat;* 7, *granulated cork packing;* 8, *bottom ring;* 9, *inlet pipe and baffle;* 10, *bottom cover;* 11, *drain plug for emptying;* 12, *inlet valve;* 13, *outlet pipe*

There still remains sufficient heat loss to warm an airing cupboard; too much heat is known to have a detrimental effect on linen. Where towel rails and radiators are run from the system in winter time when the solid fuel boiler is in use, care should be taken to disconnect them when the immersion heater is in operation.

The electric storage heater (Fig. 30) is an efficiently insulated, self-contained tank, fitted with a thermostatically controlled heating element, built to stand beneath the draining board or fitted above the kitchen sink or, where more convenient, in the bathroom. The most efficient type incorporates two heating elements: one near to the top of the container, so that 5 to 6 gallons of water may be quickly heated for such purposes as washing up, the other at the bottom, to be used when a larger quantity is required for baths or laundry purposes. The switch operates top or bottom elements as required; each has its own thermostat. This type of heater will supply hot water to a number of taps if required.

The system of heating water as it passes through a container usually involves a high electric loading, which is not suitable for domestic use. A small instantaneous heater is, however, available, which is worked in conjunction with a storage heater; from the storage heater, water is fed into a small unit and quickly brought to the boil, the current switching off automatically as soon as the water is drawn off.

COOKING STOVES

The choice of a cooking system is governed by the design of the kitchen, the size of the family and pattern of family life, and the preference of the housewife for a particular type of fuel or of cooker with which she may be familiar. So much help and information is now easily available to housewives, however, that the last point should not be given much importance; a sensible housewife will be willing to adapt herself, and to learn to use a cooker new to her, when other factors cause it to be especially suitable for her needs. In the housecraft room in a school as many different types of cookers as possible should be installed, and the pupils made familiar with each kind. It is indeed a matter of some concern that solid fuel cookers should be installed with this end in view, but instead are often used merely as space heaters, or for very occasional use when the gas or electric cookers become overcrowded. In the past, this situation no doubt arose from the fact that most solid fuel appliances were wasteful and inefficient, and difficult to regulate. In recent years, they have been so greatly improved that this reason no longer exists.

The initial cost of a *heat storage cooker* is high, and extra expenditure is entailed for installation. But if properly used the cooker is economical to run, and particularly suitable for households where a fair amount of cooking is done. These cookers depend for their efficiency on the storage and control of heat (Fig. 18). A small continuously burning fire heats a thick metal accumulating block, the heat from which is taken through conduction plates to the ovens and remaining parts of the cooker. The hot plate surface is extensive, the hottest part being directly over the fire, and is used where fast boiling is required, the remaining section being used for simmering. When not in use, the plates are covered with heavily insulated lids, so that the heat is conserved, and the kitchen not overheated. Cookery utensils must be designed to make even contact with the hot plates, and should therefore be of the heavy ground-base variety. A thermostat is fitted and provides automatic control of the rate of burning of the fire. Two ovens at least are provided, the institutional models having four or more; the hottest oven is intended to be used for baking, a medium oven for simmering, and in some models an auxiliary oven is provided for plate warming and for keeping cooked food hot. Good oven insulation ensures steady, even heat, very little of which can escape into the kitchen. Most heat storage cookers are designed to burn smokeless fuels only, and in this case only occasional sweeping of the chimney is necessary; some types will also burn bituminous coal. Because the fire is small, and the whole appliance is so heavily insulated, fuel consumption is low. The stoking and riddling of the fire, and the removal of ashes, are simplified as much as possible. The cookers are covered in vitreous enamel, available in a variety of attractive colours, which is hard wearing and easily cleaned. Bright parts are chromium plated. Cookers are available with boilers which supply constant hot water.

As its name implies, the *semi-insulated cooker* (Fig. 31) is less heavily insulated than the heat storage type; as a result, fuel consumption is higher, and the kitchen receives a greater amount of background warmth; the cooker is smaller, and less expensive. A wide choice of fuels is possible. Ovens are heated by hot air circulating inside them, or by hot air, or flue gases, circulating around them. Hot water boilers are usually incorporated; accurate air controls for the oven and for water heating are fitted. The cleaning of flues and ash removal are made as labour-saving as possible; the outside surfaces are easily cleaned and attractive in appearance. Various other features are offered by different

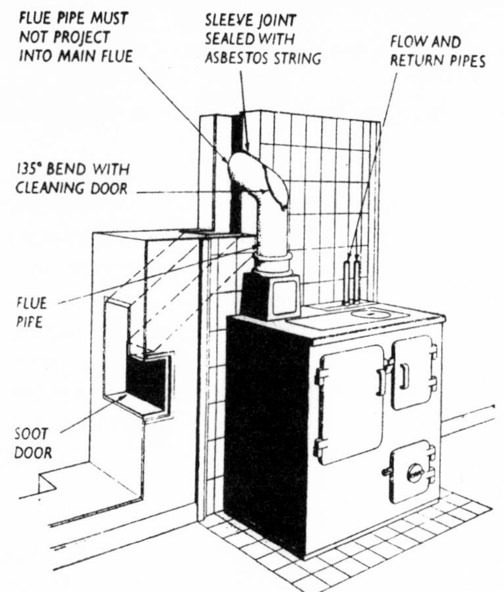

31 *A free-standing or semi-insulated cooker*

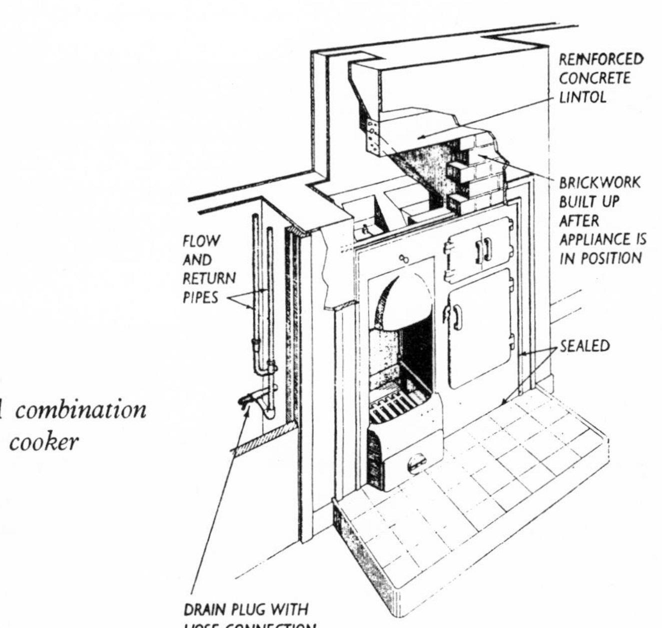

32 *A combination cooker*

manufacturers. This type of cooker for the use of solid fuel is the one most often installed in housecraft rooms in schools.

The *combination cooker* (Fig. 32) is a type which is particularly popular in the North of England, and suitable for a kitchen living-room; it provides cooking facilities, hot water and space heating by means of an open fire. The modern variety provides a cover to the fire-box for overnight burning, and will burn both coal and smokeless fuels. The oven may be to the side of the fire, with a cooler oven above for plate warming; in other models, useful where space is limited, the cooking oven is placed over the fire. This type is suitable for elderly people, and is often installed in flats which have been designed for them. A third variety of combination grate is the back-to-back appliance; in this unit, the fire heats the living-room and the cooker, which is placed behind it in the kitchen, on the other side of a partition wall; a boiler is fitted between them.

Electricity

The extreme cleanliness of cooking by electricity makes it a popular method, especially for a modern kitchen. Since the heat is produced through the medium of resistance wires, there is no flame, and no products of combustion; no dirt is therefore produced in the kitchen, the saucepans remain clean and the cooker itself is made of strong vitreous enamel, easily kept clean by wiping over with a damp cloth after use. The modern cooker is obtainable in shades to match or harmonise with kitchen colour schemes. Two or three hot plates are provided in different sizes. The enclosed type of hot plate (Fig. 34) requires flat ground-base saucepans for economical use; these make even contact with the plate and ensure good conduction of heat. A radiant hot plate (Fig. 33) with a tubular element, which glows red-hot when in use, is fitted to some cookers; from it, the heat is conveyed by radiation as well as conduction. The heat is controlled by 3-heat switches, or by simmerstat control, which provides greater variety in temperature and enables the heat to be reduced to a low degree for simmering. Most cookers have a grill boiler, which enables grilling to be done underneath the plate while boiling on top; a reflector plate is provided for use when the hot plate is required for only one purpose. The grilling compartment provides good storage space for keeping plates and dishes warm; no plate rack is necessary. The oven is thermostatically controlled and is well insulated, giving very even cooking. Many cookers have an inner glass door, so that the food may be seen when required during cooking without causing heat from the oven to escape into the kitchen. Elements are usually placed at the sides of the oven; the interior of the oven may be easily cleaned, some oven linings being lifted out in one piece for this purpose. Many cookers have a drawer beneath the oven, so that its heat is utilised for keeping food and dishes warm.

33 *Electric hot plate: radiant type*

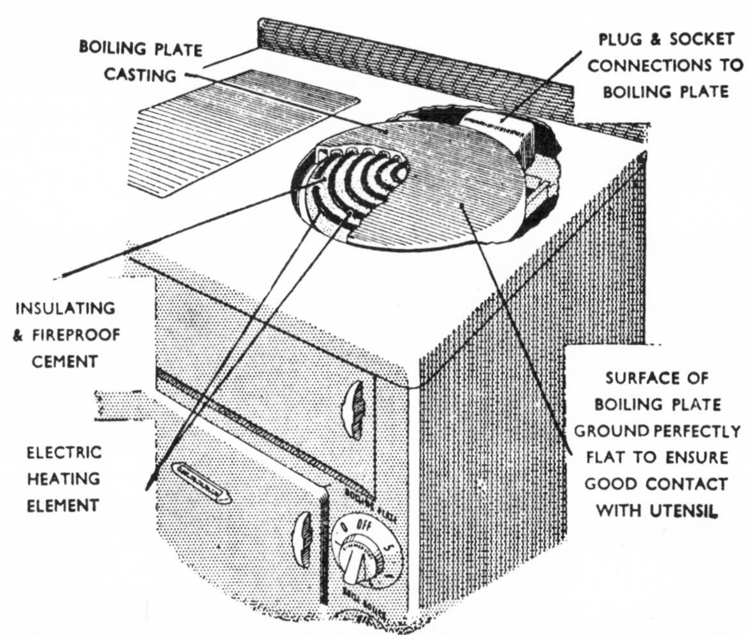

34 *Electric hot plate: enclosed type*

Some cookers are made with the oven alongside the hot plate instead of underneath; this prevents the necessity for stooping, and enables additional storage cupboards to be provided in the lower part of the cooker, and also above the oven. Another development has been to separate the hot plate and oven completely; the hot plate can then form part of a working unit, a very convenient arrangement, while the oven can be built into the wall and save space.

Automatic time control, provided with some cookers, enables the food to be left in the oven until the time when its cooking should begin; a dial is set to this time, and another for the length of cooking time required. This enables a family to return from work to a cooked meal, ready for serving. Other convenient fittings are a ringing timer, set like an alarm clock to give a reminder when cooking is finished, an electric clock fitted into the cooker, concealed tubular lighting for the hob, and floodlighting for the oven controlled by the opening of its door. A main switch for the cooker, which should be turned off when it is not in use, and for cleaning, is provided in a panel which usually contains also a plug socket for an electric kettle.

Gas

As in the case of solid fuel and electric cookers, the design of gas cookers has been improved to give attractive appearance, ease of cleaning and convenience in use. The hot plate of the cooker is fitted with 2 to 6 aerated burners which are usually varied in size. The burners may be of the ring type, or the solid centre type, and give even and easily regulated heat. Automatic ignition may be provided. Pan supports enable the saucepans to be moved about the hot plate without tiliting. Where the grill is underneath the hot plate, it has a cover to prevent overheating of the plate above; the eye-level grill is now preferred by many people, as it prevents the necessity for bending. Safety taps on the modern cooker are designed to prevent small children from turning on the gas.

The oven is thermostatically controlled; the interior is lined with enamel and easily kept clean. The burner is now usually placed at the back of the oven; automatic timing, where it is installed, will ensure that the cooker will turn itself on at any time required and for as long as required. Other additions to some of the modern gas cookers are glass doors to the ovens, kitchen clocks and strip lighting.

LIGHTING

Efficient lighting, both natural and artificial, is now understood to be an essential feature of every home; the tendency in building modern houses is to plan the aspect of living and working areas so that they have the maximum amount of sunlight, and to provide large windows. Many people, where privacy allows, prefer to leave windows unobscured by net curtains, and to pull draw curtains well aside during the day. For many of the family, the hours spent in home activities and in leisure occur after dusk, and the planning of good artificial lighting is of great importance in every part of the house. While the chief reason for this is the avoidance of eye-strain, good illumination is essential for home safety, since badly lit staircases and dark corners can often be the cause of accidents; in modern homes, it also forms part of the decoration.

Because of its much greater efficiency and convenience, electricity has superseded all other forms of lighting; older methods are, however, occasionally used for special circumstances and in some country areas. The candle, where a cotton wick is coated with layers of wax, is used mainly for decorative purposes; many sizes and varieties of coloured candles are available, and are often combined with flowers and greenery to make attractive Christmas decorations. Oil lamps are in use in remote country districts without gas or electricity; in these, a metal reservoir contains paraffin, the adjustable cotton wick is held by a burner, its flame enclosed by a glass chimney and shaded; the most modern lamp is fitted with an incandescent burner of chemical fabric, which becomes white hot and gives a strong white light; for efficient burning an oil lamp must be filled daily, and kept clean. Gas lighting, which was introduced in the early nineteenth century, was used throughout the country until the introduction of electricity; its efficiency was greatly improved and its popularity increased by the use of the incandescent mantle; a mixture of gas and air was burnt, raising the mantle to white heat and producing a steady, uniform light; ignition was simplified by the use of pilot lights.

The introduction of the vacuum lamp by Swan and Edison in 1878 marked the beginning of the use of electricity for interior lighting. In this lamp the air was pumped out of the bulb and a filament of carbon was heated to incandescence by an electric current. After some years of experiment, a more efficient filament of tungsten was discovered, and it then came into general use. The brightness of light produced by the flow of current through the filament can be varied by using lamps of different wattage, the best being gas filled. The wide choice of lamps now available includes pearl, which are useful for general purposes and produce less glare than clear glass bulbs; silica coated, for softer diffused light; and pink tinted for pleasant flattering light. Reflector lamps may be used for limited areas or points of interest; tubular lamps may be used without shades to light book cases or dressing tables; architectural lamps of tubular white glass may be used for mirrors, bedheads, pelmets and shelves. Whatever the type of lamp chosen for a room or part of a room, it should fit into the scheme of decoration, and be simply designed; fittings should be planned to obscure as little light as possible, while avoiding glare, and be easily cleaned.

Fluorescent lighting is now commonly used in offices and factories and in all kinds of public buildings; it is excellent for kitchens and all working areas of a house. In a fluorescent lamp a discharge in a low pressure of mercury vapour generates ultra-violet radiation, which acts on certain chemicals forming the "fluorescent powder" coating the sides of the tube, and causes them to glow. Tubes are 1 inch or 1½ inches in diameter, and from 1½ feet to 8 feet long, and are available in different wattages. Colours available in these lamps are daylight or colour matching, natural and de luxe warm white; where food is prepared the de luxe warm white is usually recommended. The large area of lighting surface and relatively low brightness of the lamp surface which results, succeed in reducing glare and shadows to a minimum. The lamps last longer than filament lamps, and better lighting is obtained for the same cost; the lighting is economical, since there is no heat loss. With prolonged use of fluorescent lighting, there is some possibility of the excess ultra-violet rays causing eye strain.

Lighting the House

Living-room Here most time is spent in recreation, and it is essential to provide adequate lighting for the various members of the family who may be using the room at any one time to see without eye strain. A general light from a central pendant fitting, or from wall brackets, is required, together with local lights from reading lamps in different parts of the room (Figs. 37–39). Clever use of concealed lighting for pelmets, alcoves and shelves adds to the decoration of the room. The angle-poised lamp, though not always decorative, is a valuable addition, and enables a member of the family to read or sew without disturbing viewers of television. For this room especially, it is never advisable to choose lamps of low wattage with a view to economy; lamps which are to be used for reading or sewing need to be 100 watts as a general rule.

Dining Area The dining table should be adequately lit by a pendant light, and the sideboard, or table used for serving, similarly well lit. The ceiling fitting which can be raised or lowered is useful, especially where the dining table is used also for children's homework. Dark corners in the room should be overcome by the use of wall fittings or similar arrangements.

Kitchen Fluorescent lighting is the most efficient choice, and good general lighting is essential; it should, however, be supplemented by local lights over working surfaces where necessary, and particularly over the sink; wall cupboards projecting over work surfaces should have lamps beneath them; all deep cupboards should be fitted with lights which are automatically turned out by the closing of the doors by switches on door jambs.

Hall and Staircase Lighting here adds greatly to the welcoming appearance of the hall; it must be sufficiently bright to light the staircase efficiently and help to avoid accidents, though an additional light on the stairs is usually necessary; the lights should be controlled by a two-way switch operating from the hall and from the landing (Fig. 40).

Bedrooms Here local and general lights are desirable. Beds should have reading lamps placed above them and controlled by separate switches; the general light should be controlled by a switch near the bedside in addition to one near the door. All mirrors should be well illuminated; wardrobes or fitted cupboards should have interior lights, controlled by opening and closing the doors.

Bathroom General and mirror lights are necessary, and fluorescent lighting is efficient for the purpose. Light should be controlled by the cord type of switch, or by ordinary switches placed outside the door.

Outside the House Lights at the front and back doors of a house are very useful, and should be controlled by switches inside the house; enclosed fittings protect the lamps from the weather. A garage should have at least two lights, one being over the engine of the car. A light in a greenhouse is also useful.

Chapter 7

Materials Used in the Home

WOODS

Both in the structure and in the appointments of a house, wood continues to be extensively used, and its suitability for so many purposes and variety of finishes, together with its beauty of colour and graining, make it unlikely that it will ever be superseded completely by more modern materials.

Timber is divided into two classes, hardwoods and softwoods; the distinction is a botanical one, hardwoods being derived from the broad leaf trees growing in tropical and temperate zones, and softwoods from the conifers growing in temperate and cold zones. Most hardwoods, though not all, are heavier and harder to work than softwoods; they are durable woods, popular for furniture and flooring because of their beauty. The softwoods are used mainly for house structure.

The complex cellular structure of wood assists the penetration of glue and also of liquid preservatives. As a tree grows thicker, the cells just beneath the bark divide and enlarge; annual growth rings, with which most people are familiar, are formed by the difference between spring and summer wood. In many trees it is also possible to see a darker coloured area, which is called the heartwood, in the centre of the trunk; as growth has proceeded, the cells of the heartwood have ceased to function, and its main function is to support the tree. A ring of lighter wood around it is called the sapwood; its function is to transmit water and food through its living cells (Fig. 35).

Trees are usually felled in the winter months when the absence of leaf makes the top lighter and the process easier; the ground is often hardened by frost, an advantage in transporting the felled trunks, and winter climatic conditions are not conducive to attacks by fungi, discoloration and other defects more readily developed in summer. Branches are lopped off; the tree trunks are then transported, in this country by lorry, to timber mills, where they are sawn up into planks, this process being known as the conversion of timber. The method of sawing is important, as it affects the decorative value, the amount of shrinkage and resistance to wear, while correct sawing also ensures that wood will not be wasted. Shrinkage is greatest when the wood is sawn tangentially to the circumference of the trunk (flat-sawn); logs to be used for floorboards, or other purposes where shrinkage is of particular importance, should be quarter sawn, so that the annual growth rings are at right angles to the face of the board (Fig. 36).

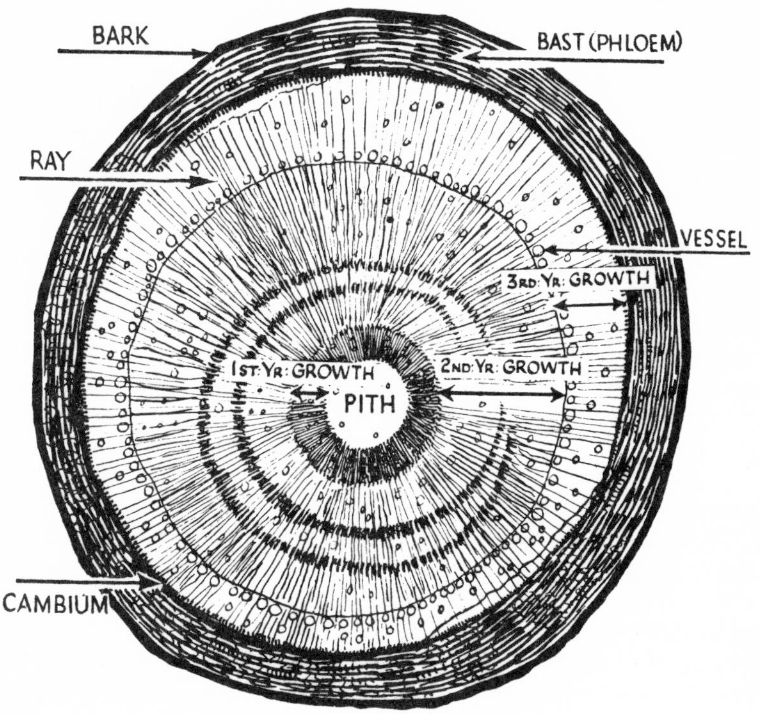

35 *The growth of wood*

Wood which has been newly sawn has a moisture content varying from 30 per cent to 200 per cent (the weight of moisture in the wood expressed as a percentage of the weight of the dry wood). Most of this moisture must be removed as soon as possible after conversion, and since shrinkage occurs during the drying process, warping of the wood may result unless the rate of drying can be carefully controlled. Two methods of removing moisture from timber are employed—air seasoning and kiln seasoning; often a combination of both methods is used. Hardwoods, which require particularly slow drying, are usually best treated in winter, softwoods in spring. In air seasoning, the wood is stacked on well-drained ground, the bottom layers raised above the ground in order to let the air circulate, and supported on foundations of brick, or creosoted wood blocks. In order to assist the circulation of air, the layers of timber are separated throughout the pile by clean dry sticks, and by varying the size and distance apart of these sticks, it is possible to control to some degree the rate of drying. The stacks are protected from the rain and from sun by weather boards or other covers. The time for drying varies according to the thickness and type of wood, softwoods requiring 2 to 4 months, and hardwoods taking about a year to dry out to a moisture content of 20 per cent, at which stage they are often transferred to a kiln for further drying. Where the wood is to be used in buildings heated by central heating, a moisture content as low

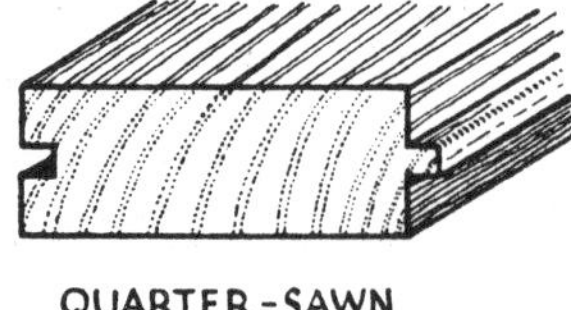

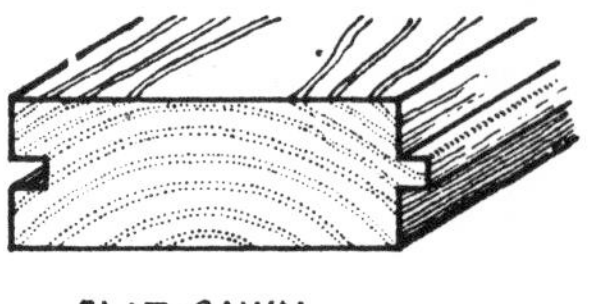

36 *Timber: quarter-sawn; flat-sawn*

as 9 to 12 per cent is necessary, and in this country the climate makes it impossible to dry it out of doors to this extent.

Careful stacking of the timber in the brick kiln is necessary; at the higher temperature, shrinkage and warping are very likely to occur, and, as in air seasoning, piling sticks are used to separate the layers. In the kiln, which is fitted with heating pipes, the temperature and humidity of the circulating air may be controlled according to the type of wood being treated, and the rate of drying suitable for it. In some kilns, natural circulation of warm air is used, and in others the air is forced to circulate by means of electrically driven fans, while steam is introduced through jets. The amount of moisture left in the wood will vary according to its ultimate use and surroundings.

Dead wood in a forest is attacked by fungi and this is a natural activity necessary to break it down and to restore value to the soil, thereby assisting propagation. Felled timber is apt to be attacked by both fungi and insects, but these need favourable conditions of moisture, temperature and air, so that if some of these factors can be controlled, the wood will be preserved. Seasoning should begin as soon as possible after sawing, so that the wood is not left lying in piles in a damp condition. If kept permanently dry, wood cannot decay, nor will completely saturated timber be attacked. It is not easy to control these factors when

37 *An example of poor lighting*

38 *The same room with good lighting*

39 *Sensible lighting for the corner of a room*

40 *A well-lighted staircase*

the timber has been put to use, and so the methods of preservation usually aim at poisoning the food supply for the fungi or insects by treating the wood with suitable preservatives. Some woods are more resistant to attack than others, and are therefore said to be durable woods. Sapwood is more liable to attack than heartwood.

Three types of preservative are used: (1) *The oily type.* The best-known is coal tar creosote, which is available cheaply, is poisonous to fungi and insects, and is practically insoluble in water; its strong smell makes it suitable mainly for wood which is to be used out of doors. Wood which has been recently treated with creosote becomes more inflammable, but this effect wears off after a few months. (2) *The water-soluble type.* In these, chemicals are dissolved in water and the resulting solutions are toxic; they penetrate the wood easily, do not stain it, and are non-inflammable; being water soluble, they are used more for dry conditions than for outdoor work. (3) *The solvent type.* In these, the poisonous chemicals are dissolved in spirit or volatile oil. The solvents penetrate the wood well, and afterwards evaporate, leaving the chemicals behind. Many patent preservatives are of this type, and are relatively expensive.

Softwoods

Softwoods in common use in this country include home-grown and Baltic pine, often known as deal; spruce, various types of fir, larch and yew. These are used, when creosoted, for outdoor work and, in the case of the best qualities, for structural work such as floor joists, ceiling rafters, doors and window frames, staircases; also for kitchen furniture, built-in furniture and furniture which is to be painted.

Hardwoods

Some of the best known hardwoods, on account of their variety of colour and graining, and strength, should be given individual consideration.

Oak is one of the most useful woods in this country, and probably the best known. Oak trees, when felled, are often 150 to 200 years old; the seasoning process must be slow, and the wood is air seasoned, sometimes for years, and then kiln seasoned at a low temperature. The resulting wood is hard and strong, and has a number of uses in house construction, outdoor work, and all kinds of furniture. The natural colour of oak varies from pale to dark brown, and it can be easily stained and polished by any of the methods in use. Other finishes, such as fuming, liming and weathering, help to give variety to oak furniture.

Beech varies in colour from almost white to reddish brown; it stains and polishes well, and is a useful timber for chair legs, tool handles, kitchen utensils and also for flooring.

Ash is a tough and elastic timber, fire resistant; it seasons well and rapidly, and is particularly useful for sports goods.

Elm, a very common wood in England, is a strong rough timber, difficult to saw; it is used for coffin boards, and, being water resistant, for weatherboards, wheel barrows and road paving blocks, as well as for boat building and for furniture.

Sycamore is a creamy, yellowish-white wood which tends to darken; it is not very durable, but is easily penetrated by preservatives. It is used for furniture, for veneers, and for kitchen utensils.

Walnut varies in colour from grey to reddish-brown; it is a highly figured wood, and very popular for furniture, taking a smooth fine finish and good polish; it is also widely used for veneers. Most of the walnut used in England is imported, and a large number of timbers which bear a superficial resemblance to it are given the name.

Mahogany, which is prolific in Nigeria, is a very strong, decorative wood, used in the eighteenth century for furniture by Chippendale, Adam, Hepplewhite and Sheraton. In recent years, some mass-produced furniture has been treated and polished to resemble mahogany, but lacks its attractive colour and fine graining.

Teak is prolific in Burma, India and the East Indies. It is a very durable wood, resistant to fungi, and can be used for outdoor work without painting; it is fire resistant, is in demand for ship building, and is used in houses for draining boards and also for furniture.

Plywood

Plywood is produced by gluing thin sheets of wood together under pressure; the result is wood which gives the maximum strength with the minimum weight, and is relatively inexpensive. It does not warp easily, and has many uses for furniture and floors. Where parquet flooring is installed, a base of plywood is often first nailed to the sub-floor; the parquet is then pinned and glued to the plywood, which helps it to maintain a flat surface unaffected by possible shrinkage of the sub-floor.

METALS

Silver

Silver is the whitest of all metals. In its early days it was more valuable than gold because of its scarcity. In Great Britain it was probably first used for jewellery, then for church vessels, later for spoons and drinking vessels; for domestic use it is mixed with copper, which does not affect its colour, but increases its toughness and hardness. Standard solid silver has 925 parts silver, 75 parts copper. Silver is called a noble metal; it stands exposure and repeated meltings. It does not tarnish with oxygen, but reacts with sulphur, forming the black tarnish silver sulphide. Silver is a very malleable metal and may be beaten and engraved. Modern uses are for tea services, spoons and forks, presentation cups; designs have been simplified, the elaborate decoration of older silver making its cleaning difficult. Although it was at one time used for coinage, "silver" coins are now made from a mixture of copper, zinc and nickel.

A hall-mark is a stamp applied to an article made of standard solid silver to denote its quality; the article must first be tested or assayed to prove that its standard is that required by law. The marking is done at an Assay Office, by a legally appointed official, and is taken throughout the world as a guarantee of the quality of British silverware. It consists of four marks stamped on the metal. The Maker's Mark gives the initial of the manufacturer. The Hall or Assay Office Mark, known also as the Town Mark or the Mark of Origin, identifies the office at which the testing was done; the London mark is the leopard's head, Chester uses the arms of the city, Birmingham an anchor, Sheffield a crown, Edinburgh a castle, Glasgow a fish, tree and bell, with a bird on the tree, Dublin a crowned harp. The Quality Mark, used by all the English offices, is the Lion Passant; Edinburgh uses a thistle flower with two leaves, Glasgow the Lion Rampant and also the thistle. These marks denote that the silver is of sterling standard. The Date Mark shows the year in which the silver was made. A letter has been taken to represent each year, which changes in London on May 29th. Each cycle has its own specially shaped letter and shield, and these vary from town to town. The older quality mark of the figure of Britannia is still in occasional use in Britain. Another mark seen is the Jubilee Mark; silver made in the year 1935 was stamped with the heads of the King and Queen to commemorate their Silver Jubilee.

Electro-Plating For this, an article of nickel or some other white metal is placed in a solution of silver salts, an electric current is passed through, and a layer of silver deposited on the article. Its value depends on the thickness of the layer; a good quality will last about 25 years, while cheaper thin layers of silver get rubbed off in time. A good quality electro plate, with a foundation of nickel, is marked E.P.N.S., Electro-Plated Nickel Silver, and the mark A.1 denotes that the article has the best guaranteed life.

Oxidised silver is useful for trinket boxes and ornaments. It consists of a layer of silver on a foundation of steel.

Sheffield Plate consists of a layer of silver sprayed on to a foundation of copper. Owing to the expense of copper, it is now seldom made.

Nickel

Nickel is a lustrous white metal, which does not tarnish in pure dry air at normal temperatures, but tarnishes when the humidity is increased; food products do not affect it, and it is used considerably for canteen ware. Its appearance is maintained by occasional rubbing. The name originated in Germany, and both the "German silver" and the "nickel silver" used for cutlery and in electro-plating are mixtures of copper, nickel and zinc, containing no silver.

Aluminium

Although the existence of the mineral salts from which aluminium is now extracted was known as far back as Roman times, many different attempts and experiments by scientists were necessary before the discoveries leading to the production of aluminium were made, and the industry itself is comparatively recent. Aluminium oxide occurs abundantly in many common rocks, which are given the name bauxite, derived from the French town of Les Baux, where they are mined. Mining is carried out by open-cast methods, or, where the bauxite is deeper, by methods similar to coal mining; it is washed, crushed, screened to reduce its bulk, and transported by ship, often to countries some considerable distance away, where aluminium works have been established. Here various chemical processes result in the extraction of the alumina or aluminium oxide in the form of white powder. Further treatment at the reduction works (where the powder is dissolved in molten cryolite, consisting of aluminium fluoride, a mineral found in Greenland) takes place by passing an electric current through the fused mixture; this liberates the oxygen and the aluminium is left.

In its pure state, aluminium is a soft metal, and to harden it it is alloyed with copper, iron or other metals. Its extreme lightness enables it to be used for many constructional purposes, for building bridges, aircraft and ships and for engineering. It is a very good conductor of electricity, and of heat, which makes it suitable for cooking utensils and hot plates. Owing to a thin protective layer of aluminium oxide which settles on it, the metal resists tarnish; this can be increased by a process known as anodising, which produces a very hard, resistant film. Other finishes given to the metal are chromium-plating, for kettles and saucepans and other cookery equipment, and painting, for store cupboards and kitchen units. It is used in the construction of many pieces of household equipment, including laundry equipment and suction cleaners, as well as small utensils. Aluminium foil is used as insulating material, and for many food wrapping purposes.

Copper and Brass

Copper is a metal of very early origin; its name originated in Cyprus. It is a very ductile and malleable metal, which can be rolled into thin sheets, drawn into fine wires, pressed or beaten. In the household its high degree of conductivity results in its extensive use in electrical wiring; it is used too for water pipes, which do not burst easily. Its attractive colour makes it popular for ornamental purposes; when used for cookery utensils its good retention of heat is of great advantage. Copper does not tarnish in pure dry air; but where sulphur is present, and in moist air, a black film slowly forms which turns to green verdigris.

A good quality brass has three parts of copper and one part of zinc, the proportion of zinc rising in inferior qualities. Its uses are for ornamental purposes mainly. The lacquering of brass and copper ornaments saves much time and energy which would otherwise be spent in cleaning them, and is advisable particularly in town atmospheres.

Iron and Steel

The knowledge and use of the mineral iron is very old. The element exists in combination with other substances from which it is separated in the blast furnace, the smelting of the ore producing what is called pig or cast iron. The industry has always depended on coal production, and iron has in its turn been used for the shafts of coal mines, and steel for the engines used to haul the coal to the surface. The industry produces cast iron and wrought iron, the latter being less brittle and more durable. Steel is made from a mixture of iron and carbon, with the addition of very small amounts of certain metals—such as nickel, manganese, tungsten, chromium—in different combinations to suit many purposes.

For domestic use, iron must be protected against rust, the red oxide of iron which forms upon it in damp air. Various methods of protection are employed, according to the use to which the iron is put; gutters and pipes outside the house are painted; kitchen equipment is given a hard and durable coat of vitreous enamel, small articles a thinner coat of enamel or tin; sheets for fencing or for roofing are sprayed or plated with a coating of zinc. When iron has been coated with another substance, care must be taken when cleaning it; both tin and zinc will wear off if treated with a coarse abrasive or very strong alkali.

The blades of knives are made from steel which is forged and ground. As ordinary steel becomes stained very readily, both kitchen knives and table cutlery are now largely made of stainless steel. Stainless steel is rustless, being made from a combination of iron and carbon with chromium. It is used for kitchen equipment of various types, especially sinks and cookery pans, and for articles such as fenders and fire irons.

Tin

Tin is a soft, lustrous and malleable metal, which is very little affected by moist air at ordinary room temperatures, and is harmless to food. The common "tin" used as a food container or cookery utensil is made of a thin sheet of iron, protected against the atmosphere, and against organic acids in foodstuffs, by a layer of tin plating. Tinfoil is used for wrapping purposes.

Chromium

Chromium is a bluish-white metal which takes a high polish and is practically unaffected by air. Because of its hardness and resistance to corrosion, chromium plating is widely used for aluminium kitchen utensils, and for metal fittings such as water and gas taps, handles of cupboards and metal parts of modern equipment.

Pewter

Old pewter is an alloy of tin and lead; modern pewter contains copper, tin and antimony. It is used for tea sets and ornaments in simple and pleasing designs.

Zinc

Zinc is a soft metal which is used as a protective coating for iron; the pails and baths made in this way have been largely superseded by plastic equipment, but galvanised iron is used for roofs and fences.

LEATHER

It is known that the skins and hides of animals were used by primitive man for clothing and for footwear. Having no special treatment to preserve them, these decayed in time; many attempts were made to find ways of making them last longer, but hundreds of years were to pass before the art of tanning, which converted the raw hides and skins into flexible and durable leather, was discovered. It was found that the toughness and strength of the substance made it suitable for many purposes other than clothing, and the leather industry has grown throughout the years and spread to many parts of the world.

In the conversion of hides into leather, certain basic processes take place. After soaking in water to make them soft and pliable, the hides are put into lime pits, where by bacterial action the roots of the hair are destroyed, so that it may be easily removed. Three main tanning processes are used today. Vegetable tanning, which until the middle of the nineteenth century was always done with oak bark, now involves the use of other materials of greater strength and special characteristics; various barks, seed pods and leaves are used, and also tannic extracts of various kinds of wood, which are convenient in use and give a uniform result. In the second method, the leather is combined with certain mineral salts, which impregnate and preserve it. The third method uses a treatment with oils and fats; this is used for chamois or buff leather. A combination of all three may be employed where suitable.

Both the hide selected and the tanning process used must be suitable for the use to which the leather will be put; tanneries therefore tend to specialise and produce leather for particular purposes. Where the salts of the metal chromium are used in the tanning process, the resulting leather, for which many kinds of hide may be used, is very resistant to water and suitable for the uppers of shoes; the soles are usually made of vegetable tanned ox hide, which combines hard wear with flexibility. Sheepskins are used for many purposes, for rugs, linings for boots and slippers, and for suede leather, which is made by smoothing the skin on the flesh side after tanning, and then dyeing and softening it; "chamois" leather is made from split sheepskin. Cow hide is used for upholstery leather, pigskin for luggage and fancy articles, Morocco leather, made from goatskin, for many fancy articles; reptile leather for the uppers of shoes and for fancy articles. The uses to which leather is put are too numerous for full description, but its value for footwear is of particular importance. It is essential for the sake of health that shoes should not trap the perspiration which continually escapes through the pores of the skin. The structure of leather is such that between its fibres are channels of air; this enables the moisture from the feet to pass through the leather and evaporate. As the air in the channels does not conduct heat readily, leather shoes help to keep the feet warm in cold weather, and cool in very hot weather.

Chapter 8

The Choice and Care of Linen and Bedding

LINEN

To most housewives, the possession of a well-stocked linen cupboard gives great satisfaction, and modern linens are so colourful and attractively designed that there is a very wide choice available to suit different incomes. The word linen is taken here to include bed linen, table linen, towels and kitchen towels; for these linen and cotton are frequently used and the advent of man-made fibres has added further variety. The amount of linen purchased for a house depends on its size and the size of the family. The advice usually given to housewives setting up house for the first time is to allow three sets of each type of linen, so that there will be one in use and one in reserve, while the third is at the laundry. This provides a rough basis, but obviously needs modification. Where linen is laundered at home there is less timelag than when it is sent to a laundry, and it is possible to manage with less. As stocks are built up over the years, the amount of each type of linen will vary according to the needs and circumstances of the particular family.

Bed Linen

Real linen sheets give excellent wear; it is one of the strongest fabrics and when well laundered one of the best in appearance. It is found by some people to be rather cold, and it is more expensive than cotton. Cotton sheets, if they are of good quality, have almost as good wearing properties and appearance, and are warmer; cheap cotton sheets are usually poor value, without much "body" when washed, and inclined to crease badly in wear. Union sheets, made from a mixture of linen and cotton, are good, but not often available. Flannelette sheets are popular with people who feel the cold badly, and are sometimes recommended for those with rheumatism. Nylon and Terylene fitted sheets are gaining in popularity, though expensive; these fibres are also blended with cotton. All sheets are available in white, or in various plain colours, or with striped or gaily patterned borders. Hems which are finished by hemstitching have a good appearance; corded hems are less expensive and harder wearing; cheap sheets often have plain machined hems. One hem is usually wider than the other, and is intended to be put at the top of the bed, a help in making it. The size of sheets is important; if too small, they are uncomfortable in use. As both single and double beds vary in width, and to some degree in length, it is wise to measure them; modern sprung mattresses, or latex foam, are deep, and the sheets must be sufficiently large to give a tuck in of at least 18 inches at the sides and bottom, and a turn down of 18 inches at the top.

Pillow cases are sold with matching sheets, or separately, their edges plain or frilled. The most practical shape, now usually adopted widely, is the housewife type; the normal size 20 × 30 inches.

Table Linen

The large white damask table cloth is now used mainly for very formal occasions. Smaller cloths, more easily laundered, are made in plain coloured linens or with striped borders, in ginghams or cotton seersucker; rayon damask has become popular because it requires no starching. Many different varieties of mats for individual place settings are available and give scope for attractive table laying. Table napkins of about 15 inches square are made to match cloths and table mats, and are largely superseding the formal dinner napkins of white cotton or linen damask, which, like the table cloths, are kept mainly for formal occasions. Afternoon tea cloths are of white or plain coloured linen, decorated with embroidery or other finishes, with matching tea napkins. Tray cloths are gradually falling into disuse, since modern heat-proof trays seldom require them.

Towels

Bath towels are made of terry towelling, a piled cotton fabric with the loops uncut; loops should be close together and even, and it is always worth while to buy a known make. A convenient size is 28 × 54 inches; the larger bath sheet is expensive to buy, cumbersome and more difficult to launder. Hand towels are now often made of the same terry towelling, in smaller sizes; the variety known as huckaback are of linen or cotton, in a special weave which is absorbent. Very small towels of this material, often embroidered, are useful for occasional guests. Both terry towelling and huckaback may be bought by the yard, and this often saves expense when equipping kitchens or cloakrooms with roller towels or small hand towels.

Tea Towels

These need to be absorbent, and linen is very much better than cotton. Terry towelling is now used for these, and tea towels of this type made by known firms are found to be excellent, not fluffy in use and very absorbent. Both kinds are made in many gay patterns and colours, fitting well into modern kitchens.

Storage of Linen

A well-ventilated cupboard with adequate shelves, about 15 inches apart and sufficiently large to take folded sheets, is very useful for the storage of linen; it should be warm and dry. Linen shelves should always be covered with material, old sheets or cotton curtains being useful for this purpose; the cover for each shelf should be attached, by rings slipped over hooks, to the back of the shelf above, and be sufficiently long to extend forward along the shelf and then fold back over the pile of linen (Fig. 41). This helps to keep the linen clean and a good colour. In many small family houses, the airing cupboard is used to store linen in regular use; in this case it should be remembered that too much heat may cause it to deteriorate, so that where the hot water cylinder is fitted in the cupboard and unlagged, it is not wise to keep the linen in this cupboard for any length of time. Articles should be piled, like things together, and in order to ensure that the linen is used in rotation, articles returned from the laundry should be replaced in the cupboard at the bottom of the pile. Small mats and tray cloths where these are used, should be kept flat, and to avoid creasing them it is often convenient to store them in a flat box. Where space in the main linen cupboard is limited, however, it is often convenient to store table linen in the drawers of a sideboard, being careful to keep the clean linen separate from that in use.

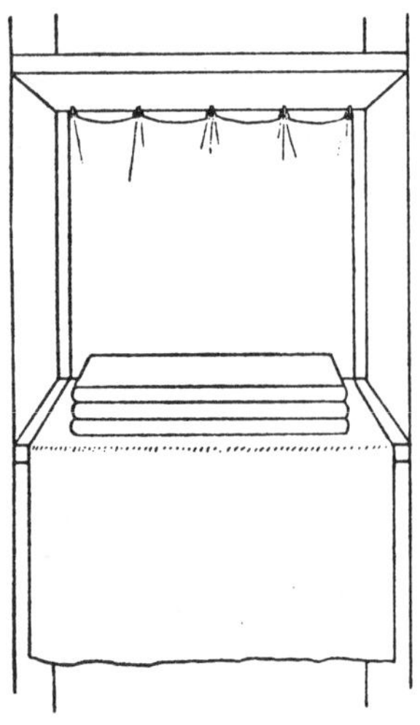

41 *A linen cupboard*

Linen Management

All linen should be clearly marked, with marking ink or woven names; special pencils are available for marking, which helps to prevent losses at commercial laundries. Repairs should be done as soon as they become necessary. Loops should always be sewn onto kitchen towels or any others which are hung up, and be large enough to be easily used.

The linen stock should be regularly replenished, and for this purpose the twice-yearly sales run by most shops are useful; often prices are reduced only because of shop soiling.

BEDS AND BEDDING

Mattresses

Suited as it is to modern bedrooms and bed-sitting rooms, the divan bed has largely superseded the larger types of bedstead; it may be obtained with or without a headboard to match existing furniture. The base of the divan is sprung and upholstered, and supports a mattress, which may be one of two types—interior sprung or made of latex foam. The interior sprung type may be made in two ways, with open springs, usually clipped together, or with pocketed springs, each enclosed in a separate cotton bag. When springs are clipped or tied together, and pressure is put on one of them, the surrounding springs sag; with pocketed springs which are not interconnected, this is avoided, and these are put into the best types of mattresses. Springs are padded with animal hair, which is expensive, or with fibre, which is cheaper; the padding is covered with a filling of wool or cotton flock or felt, or with a wool mixture. In some modern mattresses, the springs are covered with a resilient plastic foam. The outer covering is of strong linen, cotton or rayon, with handles to facilitate turning, which should be done occasionally, with care, to keep the mattress flat. Ventilation holes are provided in the box edges of the mattress.

Latex foam is made from the juice of the rubber tree, whipped into foam, and coagulated into material of cellular construction, in which the air bubbles make it porous and suitable for mattresses. It is very resilient, and gives uniform support without any possibility of sagging. The latex foam mattress is hygienic, being moth-proof, vermin-proof and dust-proof; it does not absorb moisture from the air to any appreciable extent, and may be left out of use without requiring to be aired; in use, moisture from the body is dissipated by the constant circulation of air through the mattress. The outside cover of strongly woven material protects the rubber from any deterioration caused by the action of light.

Cheap mattresses of either type should not be purchased; if sprung, they will probably contain too few springs, which will easily sag or even, in time, protrude through the outer covers; if made of latex foam, the mattress will probably be insufficiently thick to give sufficient support.

Pillows

The usual size is 20 × 30 inches. Pillows are filled with down or with feathers, and must have a down-proof cover of specially treated cotton to prevent the filling coming through it. Synthetic fibres are used for both outer cover and for filling, making particularly light and soft pillows. Pillows made of latex foam are extremely resilient, light and have the same properties as the latex foam mattress.

Eiderdowns

For these various fillings are used—pure down, feathers or mixtures—covered with down-proof material and an outer covering of a suitable fabric. Since the development in synthetic fibres, they are used with success for the outer cover and the filling, and are popular because of warmth combined with lightness, and ease of laundering.

Blankets

The best are made of pure wool, which may be moth-proofed, or of synthetic fibres, which are light, warm and easily laundered. Specially woven cellular blankets are very warm and light; merino blankets, also very light and warm, are made from wool which is particularly fine and comes from a special breed of sheep. Cotton blankets, or blankets containing some cotton, are heavy and should be avoided. All types are made in pleasant pastel colours to tone with bedroom schemes; edges may be finished by blanket stitching, or bound in satin ribbon, or with nylon.

Bedspreads

Fitted divan covers, or loose bedspreads, may be made from any fabric suitable for loose covers, which is crease resistant, washable, and harmonises with the colour scheme of the bedroom. Various designs are obtained in tufted cotton, known as candlewick, which is attractive in appearance, hangs well, shows no creasing, and is easily laundered, requiring no ironing.

Chapter 9

Detergents and Other Cleaning Agents

DETERGENTS

Since a certain amount of confusion exists over the meaning of the word detergent, it may be useful to consider that the dictionary definition of the word is cleansing agent, and to bear in mind that the oldest known manufactured detergent is soap. Soap is made by treating a fat or oil with an alkaline solution—caustic soda—producing soap and glycerine. Many different vegetable oils and some fats, from different parts of the world, are used in soap making. The resulting soap is turned into various forms according to the use for which it is designed; the molten soap is thoroughly mixed and beaten until smooth, and at this stage other ingredients are added—disinfectants, perfumes, or "builders" (compounds which assist the cleansing power of laundry soaps and soap powders). Bar soap is produced by pumping the molten soap into frames and allowing it to cool and solidify, removing it in blocks which are cut into bars and cakes, and then trimmed and stamped. Soap flakes are made by cooling the molten soap in long thin ribbons which are afterwards dried and cut. A soap powder is made by spraying the molten soap into hot air, which dries the drops and changes them to powder. To increase its efficiency as a detergent, a soap powder usually contains a mixture of alkaline-reacting salts, and may also contain fluorescent substances, and an oxidising bleach such as sodium perborate.

Dirt is attached to a fabric by being entangled in its fibres, and the coating of grease which is usually present helps to hold it in and makes its removal difficult. Often, particularly with some man-made fibres, the material acquires slight charges of electricity which attract dirt. The simplest way of cleansing is to use water alone, but without some assistance it is unable to penetrate the greasy surface and is not efficient. The use of friction or some form of agitation helps, but the addition of detergent makes the whole cleansing process easier and less harmful to the fabric; the detergent increases the wetting power of the solution and helps it to penetrate the fabric, it acts on the globules of grease, emulsifying them and preventing them from remaining in a greasy layer on the surface, and it causes the dirt to be suspended in the liquid and not to settle back again into the fabric.

A disadvantage of soap as a detergent is apparent in hard-water districts, where the salts of calcium and magnesium in the water react with the soap and form almost insoluble soaps, appearing on the water in the form of scum, and settling on the fabrics being washed. This scum carries with it traces of dirt, and gives a grey colour to white materials; it is very difficult to rinse away. Much soap is used up in overcoming this hardness before any cleansing action takes place, and for efficient and economical washing with soap it is necessary to soften the water, both for washing and at least the first rinsing.

A recent addition to some detergents is a sequestering agent which, if present in sufficient quantity, will prevent the salts responsible for hardness in the water from reacting with soap.

Synthetic detergents, when used in hard water, do not form any scum, and for this reason, and also as a result of war-time shortage of fats, and therefore of soap, their production was developed and has been tremendously extended. It has been found possible to vary their composition greatly, making them suitable for different types of fabric and different degrees of soiling.

The manufacture of these detergents is more complex than that of soap, and it uses a wide variety of raw materials, many of which are by-products of various industrial processes. For the housewife, the important factor is to understand the differences in composition of the various brands on the market in such a way that she may be discriminating in selecting them for different purposes; some of the wording used in advertisements is misleading and needs modification.

Synthetic detergents are available in liquid or powered form, and may be classified as unbuilt, lightly built or heavily built detergents. In the unbuilt or lightly built, the amount of alkali is kept to a minimum, which makes them suitable for washing woollens and delicate fabrics. The liquid detergents are generally unbuilt, and lightly built powders are those specially recommended for babies' garments and all fabrics requiring gentle washing at low temperature. The heavily built detergents are intended primarily for the cleansing of strong fabrics at high temperature. The builders which they contain have several functions, assisting the efficient removal and suspension of the dirt, increasing the alkalinity of the product, and its consequent effect on grease; mild bleaches of the sodium perborate type are added to assist removal of stains. Almost all modern commercial detergents contain fluorescent substances which simulate whiteness, and give white cellulosic fabrics an "intense" whiteness. With coloured articles, two effects are observable; pastel colours are dulled, while deeper colours are given an added brightness.

Most synthetic detergents form lather in hard and in soft water, and this property has some advantages. To some extent it controls the amount of detergent used by a housewife, since without it there is danger of using too much; the lather makes the effect of friction or agitation gentler, which is of particular importance in the case of wool; in the cleaning of carpets and upholstery, the foam settling on the surface assists in adequate rinsing without making the article too wet. The disadvantage of a large amount of persistent foaming is experienced at sewage works; it may be due to the detergent itself or to a foaming agent, and is not readily removed. The desirability of overcoming this problem has been stressed.

The effects of soapless detergents on the skin have not been found to be appreciable; where irritation or sensitiveness occurs, it is usually found to be the result of using too strong solutions, or of keeping the hands in them for long periods. Any solution which emulsifies grease will tend to dry the natural oils of the skin, and this will occur especially where the heavily built alkaline detergents are concerned.

The strong emulsifying power of the heavily built detergents necessitates care in their use in washing machines; there is some danger to the lubrication of the machine, and a detrimental effect may occur to the rubber rollers of the wringer; both effects may be found over a long period of use, and on this account many housewives prefer to use soap in some form for this purpose.

There is little difference in the principle of cleaning all hard surfaces in a house from that of cleansing fabrics, the important point being to select a cleaning agent which will be efficient without in any way damaging the surface being cleaned. The simplest method is to wash it, where suitable, in warm or hot water alone. Where the dirt is held by grease, however, the cleaning is made easier and more effective by the addition of friction, a grease emulsifier, or a grease solvent, or by a combination of some or all types of cleanser. The emulsifiers most often in use in the household are soap in one of its forms, synthetic detergents and ammonia; solvents are paraffin, turpentine, methylated spirits and carbon tetrachloride.

In the modern home, the nature of the surfaces found is such that less and less friction is necessary for cleaning; iron and steel surfaces of kitchen equipment have been replaced by hard, smooth vitreous enamel; galvanised iron pails and baths are being replaced by plastic ones; metal goods are plated with chromium, or made of stainless steel or some other stainless metal, or lacquered to prevent tarnishing; white wooden surfaces requiring to be scrubbed have been superseded by laminated plastic. When friction is necessary and harmless to the surface being treated, it is applied by means of an abrasive, a substance which will scrape off dirt. The hardest abrasives, coarse steel wool made by entangling fine ribbons of steel together, sand, emery powder and emery paper, are now seldom required; a medium abrasive, such as fine steel wool, is useful for hard surfaces which have become stained or very dirty; it is liable to scratch and should be used with soap, when its abrasive action will be softened. Other medium abrasives, such as pumice powder, from a rock of volcanic origin, and bath brick, a mixture of sand and clay from a river bed in Somerset, have been used for hard metals such as steel knives, but are falling into disuse, since most housewives find one commercial abrasive powder quite adequate for all needs. The two fine abrasives, used nowadays generally as parts of commercial cleaners, are whitening, which consists of powdered chalk, prepared by precipitation, and jeweller's rouge, which is usually a carefully prepared fine red iron oxide.

The commercial scouring powder contains an abrasive which may be fine or medium, an emulsifier in the form of soap or synthetic detergent and possibly a bleach. Abrasives in paste form are also available, and, because of their smooth consistency, are preferable for surfaces likely to scratch; in these the abrasive is fine, and it is combined with an emulsifier and solvent, and possibly some disinfectant. Because the cleaning action of these commercial preparations does not rely on friction alone, it is gentler than the old abrasive powders, acts readily on grease and removes the dirt quickly and efficiently.

A number of surfaces in the house are not improved by abrasive action, and may be effectively cleaned without it. In the cleaning of painted wood, for example, the gentler methods will help the paint to last in good condition; warm water and an emulsifier, such as ammonia or a lightly built or unbuilt detergent, so that excess alkali is avoided, is an effective method. In town districts, outdoor paint becomes exceedingly dirty; here the use of paraffin in the washing water dissolves the grease and helps the removal of dirt; it also helps to counteract blistering. Paraffin may be used also for dark-coloured indoor paint, which is apt to show streakiness if cleaned with soap.

Linoleum, owing to the nature of its composition, is another surface which should not be scrubbed or treated with an abrasive. When it requires washing, a detergent solution will be effective, while marks can often be removed by a solvent such as paraffin or turpentine. When possible, the washing of linoleum should be avoided, and polish applied regularly to keep it in good condition.

The cleaning of metals presents special problems, for, if not lacquered, they form tarnish, a film of discoloration on the surface,

42 *A table laid for dinner*

43 *A table laid for breakfast or high tea*

44 *A breakfast tray*

45 *Afternoon tea*

which is a chemical composition with constituents in the air or in certain foods. Moisture increases the tendency to tarnish, and damp foggy air has a particularly bad effect. The tarnishes which form may be basic carbonates or sulphates, oxides, chlorides or sulphides. The method of removing them is based on one or both of two factors. The first is that the tarnish may be removed mechanically by the use of an abrasive; care must be taken to choose a suitable abrasive according to the hardness of the metal, for scratching will harm it and spoil its appearance. The second factor is that tarnish may be removed by an acid, being soluble in it; again great care is necessary. Mineral acids such as hydrochloric and sulphuric would readily remove some tarnish, but at the expense of the metal itself, which they might attack; they are therefore never used except in extreme cases of neglect, when dilute hydrochloric acid, bought as spirits of salt, may be used, provided it is followed by *immediate* and *thorough* washing and rinsing. The organic acids, such as citric and acetic, available to the housewife in lemon juice and vinegar, are less harmful in their effect, and are useful for removing tarnish from engraved or embossed ornamental brass or copper, where a commercial metal polish is difficult to remove from the indentations. Where salt is used with the acid, a weak solution of hydrochloric acid is formed, the salt also giving slight abrasive action. The washing of the ornament with water containing soap or soda, and rinsing, should always immediately follow the treatment; this counteracts the effect of the acid; if it is omitted, poisonous salts will form on the metal, and retarnishing occur very quickly. When brass or copper has been used for cooking utensils, as in the case of a preserving pan, it is always preferable to clean with a soft abrasive only.

When a metal is tarnished, a film of grease is usually present. The commercial polishes suitable for ornamental brass or copper contain a fine abrasive and mild organic acid, and to remove the grease an emulsifier is added, together with a quick-drying solvent such as paraffin, turpentine or methylated spirit. The best preparation for silver cleaning has a basis of whitening and jeweller's rouge; when it is made into a liquid polish, ammonia, a detergent and methylated spirit are usually added; commercial powders, made from fine abrasives only, may be mixed with water, ammonia or methylated spirit at the time of use. Metal cleaning cloths have been impregnated with fine abrasive suitable for the particular metal; commercial wadding is impregnated with the ingredients used in metal polishes and is in a convenient form for use.

Two chemical methods for cleaning silver are useful in the home, and the first is inexpensive (see p. 120). Here, in the aluminium soda method, soda reacts with the aluminium to form hydrogen, which combines with the silver sulphide of the tarnish to form hydrogen sulphide. The second method involves the use of a commercial solution into which the silver is dipped; the solution contains a detergent coupled with an acid solution of thiourea, an organic compound which also removes sulphur from the tarnish, forming hydrogen sulphide.

POLISHES

The polishing of surfaces in a house achieves more than the production of sheen, popular because of its good appearance. Owing to the constituents used in polishes, they succeed in removing the film of dirt which is fixed with moisture or grease, and which dusting alone does not remove. In the case of wood which has not been sealed in any way, the polish "feeds" and protects it, helping to prevent splitting or cracking from dryness. Because of the hard smooth surface resulting from the use of polish, the surface will resist dirt. The polishes which have in the past been widely used for wood surfaces have had as their basis a wax, such as beeswax, dissolved in a solvent such as turpentine. For a good result, these required hard rubbing in application and in polishing. Improvements have been made by many manufacturers which lighten this work, lengthen the time for which the polish is effective, and result in a greater variety of types of polish to suit the modern surfaces found in a house.

Floor Polishes

The modern paste polish suitable for wooden floors is made from fine waxes and spirit solvents which spread easily and leave a high film which will resist soiling and marking from traffic. Antiseptics and colouring matter are often added. Paste floor polish can also be made in liquid form, which has the advantage of being easier to spread and is useful for large areas. Rubber and thermoplastic floorings are, however, softened and damaged by spirit solvents, and this fact led to the manufacture of emulsion polishes which contain no spirit, but in which the particles of wax are emulsified in water; these *water wax* polishes are made in both paste and liquid form, and are suitable for wood and for the more modern surfaces. When the polish has been spread, the water evaporates, leaving a thin, even coat of wax on the surface, which, when polished, produces a sheen.

A further development in this type of polish is what is described as a self-polishing or no-rub variety, which dries with a sheen, little or no rubbing being necessary. The protective surface obtained lasts for some considerable time without further applications. Many of the modern floor polishes, both in paste and liquid form, contain ingredients incorporated to prevent the floor from becoming dangerously slippery; they are described as non-slip polishes.

New floors will be more easily maintained if before polishing they are treated with a sealing liquid. These preparations contain drying oils and resins, which penetrate the surface; upon drying, they form a hard coat or seal which protects the floor against dirt and marks from wear. Where a surface which has previously been polished is to be treated with a sealer, all dirt and old waxes must be first removed. The sealer is left to dry, when a second coat is usually advisable. The floor is then maintained with occasional applications of polish in the usual way.

Furniture Polishes

Many modern polishes are suitable for both floors and furniture, but some types of wax polish are too heavy for furniture, and are liable to darken or discolour it. Polishes which are intended for furniture only are often in the form of a cream. The basic composition of this is similar to other wax polishes, but is in a form easy to apply to highly polished surfaces without smearing.

Silicones in Polishes

The silicones are a group of synthetic chemicals which are highly water-repellent. When polishes containing them have been applied to surfaces, a high sheen is obtained which is resistant to finger marking and other marks; dirt is unable to adhere readily. Silicones may be incorporated into polishes of both the solvent and emulsion types; the polish is easier to spread evenly, there is less tendency for the wax to smear, and the surface will resist heat and sunlight. Some polishes incorporate the silicone fluid as their main ingredient, though a little wax may be added to improve the effect on scratched surfaces. Others are mainly composed of waxes, but some silicone is added.

Such is the variety of materials used for floorings and other surfaces that where there is doubt about the suitability of polishes, information from the manufacturer of the surface material should be obtained. Reliable manufacturers of polishes publish useful information about their products, and are willing to give technical advice whenever it is required.

Chapter 10

Cleaning and Maintenance in the Home

EQUIPMENT

The increasing use of electrical cleaning equipment makes it unnecessary to provide many brooms and brushes in the modern house. There will, however, be at least one floor surface in the house for which a broom will be required for daily sweeping. Since in all probability only one need be procured, the long-handled sweeping brush should be of the best possible quality. Real horsehair is now often replaced by fibre, or a mixture of fibre or hair, or by synthetic bristles; the bristles should be thick and pliable, the head and handle finished so as to be smooth and comfortable to hold. A short-handled brush, made from materials similar to those of the broom, is essential for collecting dust, together with a dustpan of enamel or of plastic.

Even where suction-cleaning attachments are regularly used for the thorough cleaning of rooms, some type of wall brush is also useful for the more frequent attention to corners, around electric light fittings and any places where cobwebs are liable to collect. Wall brushes vary from comparatively heavy varieties with extendible handles, useful for large high rooms, to the light inexpensive type on bamboo handles, often sufficient for the average house. These brushes should always be freed from fluff after use, washed regularly and stored, either by hanging from hooks or with the head of the broom supported, so that no weight rests on the bristles.

For the cleaning of carpets and rugs without electrical equipment, stiff brooms and short stiff brushes are necessary. Where too frequent cleaning with a suction cleaner is inadvisable, a carpet sweeper is a convenient piece of equipment for the daily removal of crumbs or dust. By means of a revolving brush, the dust is swept into two dust containers and collected as the sweeper is used. Modern carpet sweepers are finished in attractive colours; it is always advisable to buy a good make.

Smaller brushes for kitchen use include scrubbing brushes, used less frequently in modern kitchens, and vegetable brushes, of which several types are available, including one of plastic.

Inexpensive floor dusting mops for use on polished floors are made of cotton which may be impregnated with oil to absorb dust. For the washing of floors and other smooth surfaces, sponge mops, which are very absorbent, are useful; these usually have some device for squeezing out the water without wetting the hands.

Electric Cleaning Equipment

The suction cleaner is so thorough for carpet cleaning, and so labour saving and clean in use, that most housewives try to buy one as soon as possible, often helped by the hire purchase system. The many different varieties which are manufactured work on the same basic

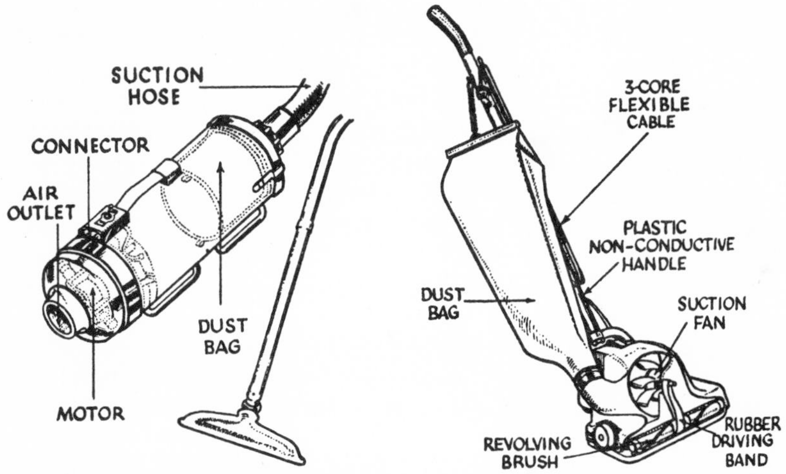

46 *The two main types of suction cleaners*

principle. A revolving fan driven by an electric motor draws air into the machine by suction, and provided that the suction opening is in close contact with the surface to be cleaned, dirt and grit are extracted from it and drawn with the air into the dust bag. As modern cleaners are automatically adjusted to the height of the pile of the carpet, the necessary close contact is easily achieved. The dust bag is made of specially woven cotton or other suitable fabric, which retains the dust while allowing the air to pass through it. Frequent emptying is essential, for if the bag becomes full of dust the air is unable to pass through the fabric and the efficiency of the suction will be reduced. Some cleaners have a disposable paper bag within the outer fabric bag.

There are two main types of suction cleaners (Fig. 46), one type relying on suction alone and the other incorporating a revolving brush and agitator. The first, cylindrical in shape, is light and easily and conveniently carried from room to room or upstairs. The dust bag is situated inside the body of the cleaner and is easily removable for cleaning from the suction end; the air passes through the bag and out of the cleaner at its other end. The cleaning is achieved by screwing a flexible tube into the suction end of the cleaner, attaching extension metal tubes to it and then the nozzle suitable for the particular surface to be cleaned, the large smooth nozzle being intended for carpet cleaning.

The second type is an upright cleaner with an outside bag, and a handle which is fitted with a rubber grip, and is easily moved into different positions: upright for storage, at a convenient angle for general use, and very low for cleaning under furniture. The agitator and brush help the removal of dirt and grit which has become embedded in the pile of the carpet. This type of cleaner is particularly suitable where there are large areas of carpet to be cleaned; it is, however, heavier than the cylindrical type for taking upstairs.

The attachments which may be purchased with suction cleaners for the cleaning of surfaces other than carpets are similar in type. A long shaped brush for the cleaning of walls and smooth floors, a small brush or nozzle for the cleaning of upholstered furniture, a round dusting brush for general dusting purposes and a crevice tool for reaching down the backs of chair cushions and similar awkward corners are the most usual kinds supplied. Some cleaners also have a spraying attachment for the shampooing of carpets, or for spraying an insecticide solution. Modern cleaning attachments are often made of plastic material. From time to time, manufacturers introduce improvements into their particular cleaners; an example is the paper dust bag, already mentioned, which is easily removed and makes the disposal of dust much cleaner in operation.

Floor Polishers

As both wooden floors and many of the newer surfaces require to be maintained by polishing, an electric floor polisher may save much time and labour in a modern house or in an institutional building where there are larger areas to be maintained. The polisher is fitted underneath with revolving brushes which are driven electrically; when the polish has been applied by hand or by means of spraying, the brushes work it thoroughly over the surface with very little effort by the worker. Extra pads of felt or lambswool are supplied to give final finish; some polishers may also be used on furniture. Some types of electric suction cleaner can also be adjusted for polishing.

Plastic Cleaning Equipment

Pails and jugs and bowls of various shapes and sizes for washing-up, for washing household surfaces and for laundry-work are often manufactured from plastics; these are light and convenient for use, easily kept clean and unbreakable. For laundry purposes they are especially suitable, as enamelled bowls, which chip in wear, tend to cause iron-mould stains to develop on fabrics. Their different colours fit well into modern kitchens and help in distinguishing equipment intended for specific uses.

ROUTINE

In an age when the advance of technology has done so much to lighten the burden of the housewife, the aim of home management is to look after the needs of the family with the least possible expenditure of time and labour so that the housewife, without becoming unduly fatigued, may have time to live a full life in other ways. In the days when many crafts were carried on at home, and when houses and families were larger, a woman's activities centred around the home and the rearing of children. Now families and houses are smaller; surfaces which are easily and quickly cleaned have replaced the older ones which required more laborious attention; more and more commodities are bought from commercial sources. Yet careful planning of the work of the home, and good methods, are necessary, perhaps more than ever before, so that time, very precious to a modern housewife, is not wasted.

The aim in this section on cleaning and maintenance is to give concise directions for cleaning the surfaces most often present in a modern house. Since, even with modern equipment, lack of a plan is likely to lead to confusion and waste of time, the order of routine cleaning is of fundamental importance.

Daily Cleaning

The daily work in a house consists of ventilation, general tidying and removal of dust from all surfaces which can be reached by hand. The order of work depends upon the fact that processes which are likely to raise dust must be done first. Where there is a carpet, it is usually inadvisable to suction clean it more than once or twice a week; the use of carpet sweepers or brushes does raise dust and therefore should precede general dusting of other surfaces. Where a suction cleaner is to be used, however, no dust is raised, and the carpet should be cleaned last so that its final appearance is immaculate.

The order given for daily cleaning is suitable when no suction cleaner is used.

Living-room, Bedroom or Bed-sitting Room

1. Ventilate the room. In the case of a bedroom, the bed should be stripped and windows opened wide by the occupant before leaving each morning. Remove old newspapers, ash-trays, waste-paper baskets, flowers needing attention and generally tidy the room. Make the bed.
2. Close windows before raising dust. Clear out and re-lay fire or, if it is continuously burning, rake and remove ashes and regulate air control.
3. Clean the carpet and rugs, sweep or mop the surround. Where there is no carpet, sweep the floor.
4. While dust is settling, clean and put away sweeping equipment, attend to flowers, etc.
5. Dust all ledges and furniture as high as the hands can reach. Tidy and arrange the room; open the windows.

Bathroom and Lavatory

1. Sweep the floor.
2. Remove dust from all ledges and surfaces.
3. Clean the washbasin, bath and lavatory pan. See that towels, etc., are hanging tidily.
4. Attend to the floor either with a wet mop or polishing mop.

Special Cleaning

The habit of giving a complete turn-out of each room in the house at weekly intervals is, for various reasons, changing in most households. The thoroughness of cleaning with electrical cleaning equipment makes the work less frequently necessary; surfaces which required frequent special cleaning, such as ornamental metals, are present to a lesser extent in modern homes, and where they are used they are often lacquered; modern polishes, both for furniture and floors, have a more lasting effect than older types. The majority of housewives, therefore, tend to give daily cleaning, with special attention to the surfaces which require it, in rotation. From time to time, however, a complete special cleaning of a room is both necessary and gives satisfaction to the worker; its frequency depends entirely upon circumstances. The order of work in special cleaning depends on whether a suction cleaner and its attachments are available for all the work, in which case no dust is raised, or for the carpet only, or in high rooms only for those surfaces which can be reached with the cleaning attachments.

Where ceiling and walls are to be swept with a wall brush, dust will fall onto the upholstered furniture unless it is protected; it should therefore, together with open book shelves, be cleaned and then covered with a dust sheet before the heavy cleaning begins. Not many households possess more than one dust sheet; where more are available, it is of course possible to clean and cover all furniture. In some cases it may be convenient to remove small articles of furniture from the room. When several rooms are to be cleaned on the same day, and where they are close together, the same type of work should be completed in all the rooms, at each stage, rather than finishing one room before beginning another.

Living-room, Bedroom or Bed-sitting Room

A. Where a Suction Cleaner is Available for the Carpet only

1. Ventilate the room; strip and air the bed. Tidy the room as in daily cleaning, removing articles to be cleaned elsewhere.
2. Using a stiff brush, brush the mattress; make the bed and cover. Brush the upholstered furniture; dust small ornaments and place them on a chair; group furniture together and cover. Dust and cover open bookshelves.
3. Close windows. Attend to the fireplace and remove ashes.
4. Using a ceiling or wall brush, sweep walls and ceiling; where complete sweeping is unnecessary, attend to corners likely to collect cobwebs. Sweep the floor surrounding the carpet, or the complete floor where there is no carpet.
5. While dust settles, clean and put away brushes; clean small articles which require washing, clean metal ornaments, attend to flowers, etc.
6. Using a duster in each hand, dust the room, including all ledges, tops of cupboards, and furniture without upholstery. Remove dust sheets carefully and shake outside.
7. Surfaces requiring to be washed: clean the paintwork; where special cleaning is done regularly, a section of paint should be cleaned each time, but marks should be removed from all surfaces, e.g. finger marks from door, dirty marks on window ledges, etc. Wash the tiles; clean the windows, mirrors, electric light fittings.
8. Surfaces requiring to be polished: polish a selection of furniture; polish hearth where necessary; polish the floor or carpet surround.
9. Suction clean the carpet. Remove all cleaning equipment.
10. Return metal and small articles; arrange furniture; open windows.

B. Where a Suction Cleaner and Attachments are Used for All the Work

No dust sheets are required. In using the suction cleaner, each attachment should be used for all its suitable purposes while it is in position.

1. Tidy room etc., as before.
2. Suction clean the mattress; make the bed.
3. Close windows; attend to fireplace.
4. With the appropriate attachments, clean all surfaces; curtains and upholstered furniture with upholstery nozzle or brush; ceiling walls, and floor or surround with the wall and floor brush; picture rail, ledges, etc., with small dusting brush; edges of fitted carpet and crevices of upholstery with the crevice tool.
5. Dust any surfaces remaining. Attend to metals, flowers, etc.
6. Attend to surfaces requiring to be washed, as in Method A.
7. Attend to surfaces requiring to be polished, as in Method A.
8. Suction clean the carpet; return small articles; arrange furniture, open window.

Bathroom and Lavatory

1. Pour boiling water containing soda and disinfectant down all waste pipes. (Avoid pouring straight from a kettle as this may crack porcelain.)
2. Close window, remove towels and toilet equipment. Sweep ceiling, walls, floor.
3. Clean bath and wash basin, using paste or fine abrasive; clean rubber plugs with turpentine; wash tiles; rub all chromium fittings with clean dry duster. Clean necessary paintwork, window, mirror, glass shelves, cork mat.
4. Clean the lavatory pan. Brush thoroughly with lavatory brush; wash outside seat and rim of pan with special lavatory cloth and hot water; flush pan.
5. Replace toilet equipment and towels. Wash or polish the floor according to type.
6. Attend to equipment. Lavatory brush and cloth should be washed in hot water containing disinfectant, and hung to dry, preferably outside.

SPRING CLEANING

Where electrical equipment is in regular use, spring cleaning, which used to entail much hard work and some measure of discomfort for the family while it was being done, is no longer necessary to the same extent. Certain pieces of work which are done only occasionally are carried out with the arrival of fine weather in the spring, though it may of course be necessary at other times also. Redecoration of the house usually takes place in the spring; washing of soft furnishings, sponging of upholstery and carpets, turning out drawers and cupboards and washing surfaces which are usually polished, are all most conveniently done when the weather is likely to assist the drying. Directions for the occasional cleaning of surfaces are given when these differ from regular cleaning.

THE CLEANING OF SURFACES

Wood Furniture and Fittings

Wood and Painted Wood Dust thoroughly. Wash thoroughly with warm water and a mild detergent, using a sponge cloth; an old nailbrush or toothbrush may be used for crevices. Stubborn marks may be removed with a fine paste abrasive. Rinse well in clean warm water, and dry with the sponge well wrung out. Avoid very hot water, strong alkali, and any cleaning agent likely to scratch the paint.

Outdoor Paint Wash with warm water containing paraffin—1 tablespoonful in ½ pail of water. Rinse in clear warm water.

Polished Wood (Wax or oil polished) Dust thoroughly. Apply a small quantity of furniture cream or wax polish suitable for furniture, and rub in thoroughly. Polish with clean, soft dusters.

French Polished Wood Wash with vinegar and water—1 tablespoon to 1 pint—to remove sticky marks, using a sponge cloth or leather. Dry and polish with a soft duster. French polish should not require further treatment unless it is in poor condition, when a little furniture cream may be used.

Removal of Heat Marks or Water Marks from polished wood. Apply, very lightly, a small quantity of metal polish, and polish off immediately. Avoid rubbing in the metal polish, or the surface of the wood will be spoilt.

Occasional Cleaning of Polished Wood Wash in warm soapy water, or vinegar and water, using a sponge cloth or wash leather. Rinse well, dry thoroughly.

Floors and Floor Coverings

Polished Wood Floor Spread the wax polish evenly over the surface, rubbing it in well; if convenient, leave it to dry. Buff well with a weighted polisher, or with an electric polisher.

Occasional Cleaning Remove old wax and dirt from the floor with a pad of fine steel wool and turpentine or a commercial cleaning solvent. Re-polish floor.

Cork Floor As for polished wood, using a water-wax emulsion for easy spreading.

Rubber Floor, Thermoplastic Tiles, Asphalt and Composition Floorings Wash the floor with warm water and detergent, rinse and dry. Use a water-wax emulsion polish; avoid the use of a spirit solvent or any

polish which contains it. Special polishes are often recommended by manufacturers, whose instructions should always be followed.
Tiles, Terrazzo and other Hard Floorings Scrub with warm water and detergent; rinse thoroughly; dry with well wrung-out cloth.
Linoleum Wash with warm water, using a detergent if necessary; avoid the use of a scrubbing brush. Rinse and dry. Stubborn marks may be removed with paraffin or turpentine. Polish with any good floor polish.

Carpets and Rugs

Remove all dust from the carpet by brushing or suction cleaning. Prepare two bowls, one containing warm water with a mild soapless detergent, the other containing rinsing water of the same temperature. Clean a section of the carpet at a time by sprinkling the detergent solution lightly and evenly over the surface with a soft laundry brush and brushing the way of the pile; rinse well with a non-fluffy cloth wrung out of the rinsing water; finally, rub the way of the pile with a dry cloth. Continue, making sure that each section cleaned overlaps the previous section. Leave the carpet to dry, ventilating the room thoroughly. Avoid putting funiture onto damp carpet, or protect it by slipping pieces of card beneath the legs of furniture, otherwise iron-mould stains may occur. Small rugs may be hung up to dry over a clothes dryer or outdoor line, care being taken to keep the edges straight.

Metals

Ornamental Brass and Copper Dust, and if very dirty wash in hot soapy water, rinse and dry. Remove tarnish by applying a little metal polish with a rag, or with impregnated wadding; polish with a soft dry cloth, using a brush for crevices. There is an alternative method which is useful for embossed or engraved ornaments when metal polish is difficult to remove completely. Prepare a bowl of hot water, containing a little soda, or detergent. Rub the ornament with a piece of cut lemon dipped into salt, or with a rag moistened with vinegar and dipped in salt; wash each section, immediately after treatment, in the water; finally rinse in clean hot water, and dry and polish with a clean soft cloth. When brass or copper ornaments have been lacquered, avoid the use of a commercial polish or abrasive. Clean by washing in soapy water, rinsing and drying.
Silver Remove tarnish with a liquid silver polish, or impregnated wadding, or a paste of plate powder and water, methylated spirit or ammonia; or rub with an impregnated silver cleaning cloth. Polish with soft cloth. Silver used for food must be washed, rinsed and dried.

The aluminium soda method of cleaning silver is suitable for any silver or silver-plated article which may be put into boiling water, and is particularly useful for table silver, where commercial polish is apt to be difficult to remove from between the prongs of forks. It should be noted that it has no effect on cutlery made from other white metals. Cover the bottom of an enamel bowl with a clean net cloth, with its corners hanging over the edge of the bowl; put silver on the cloth, and place some aluminium milk bottle tops or any old aluminium article in contact with the silver; add a lump of soda or about a tablespoonful. Pour boiling water over the silver until it is completely covered; leave about 3 minutes. Lift by the net cloth onto a draining tray; remove the aluminium; rinse silver thoroughly in clean boiling or very hot water, dry with a linen cloth and polish with a clean soft cloth.

Pewter Wash in hot water and detergent, rinse and dry. Polish with a little methylated spirit, or a liquid pewter polish; finish with a soft cloth. Old pewter is often preferred unpolished, in which case wash in water with detergent and scour well with an abrasive.

Chromium Wash and dry; rub hard with a soft duster. Neglected chromium may be cleaned with a little methylated spirit, or with a commercial polish suitable for chromium.

Soft Furnishings

Upholstery Brush with a stiff upholstery or other suitable brush, or clean with the attachments of a suction cleaner.

Occasional Cleaning After removing dust, sponge the upholstery with a solution of mild soapless detergent and warm water, cleaning a section at a time and rinsing thoroughly; avoid making the upholstery very wet. Finally rub with a dry cloth, and finish drying in a current of air. Greasy patches on armchairs may be cleaned by applying a paste of carbon tetrachloride and fullers' earth, covering with a cloth and leaving for some hours; the paste should then be removed by thorough brushing.

Leather Furniture Remove surface dust; if the leather is dirty, it may be washed in warm soapy water, rinsed and dried, or cleaned with a mixture of two parts of linseed oil to one part of vinegar. Apply a little furniture cream or polish; rub in thoroughly and polish with clean soft dusters, taking care to remove the polish completely so that it cannot mark clothing. Stains from leather furniture may be removed with a grease solvent, which should be tried with care, in case of spoiling colour.

KITCHEN HOUSECRAFT

Cooking Stoves

The use of vitreous enamel has greatly simplified the cleaning of all cookers. After use, the cooker should be wiped over, while it is still hot, with a damp cloth; if this is always done, special cleaning will be necessary less frequently.

Gas Cooker Prepare hot water and detergent; avoid using strong soda solution. Remove all movable parts, noticing their position on the cooker; clean the burners, without putting them into the water unless really necessary; leave the other parts to soak while the remainder of cooker is being cleaned. Beginning with the inside of the oven, and then working from the top downwards on the outside of the cooker, wash the enamel surfaces with hot water and detergent, using a paste abrasive where necessary. Should grease be burnt onto the surface of the oven, a proprietary cleaner may be used, following the directions carefully, and working from the back towards the front of the oven. Rinse and dry the enamel. Clean, rinse and dry all movable parts; replace in position. Light all burners for a few minutes to test and to finish drying the cooker.

Electric Cooker Turn off the electric current at the main switch before cleaning. Raise the hob of the cooker; in some cookers this may be lifted off for ease of cleaning. Remove the hot plates; any deposit should be removed with steel wool. Clean the inside of the oven, then the outside of the cooker, by washing the enamel with hot water and detergent; in some cookers the oven lining may be lifted out for cleaning. Any obstinate grease marks should be removed with a paste abrasive or pad of fine steel wool and soap. Avoid splashing the electric sockets. Rinse and dry the enamel; replace hot-plates.

Kitchen Sink

Modern sinks of vitreous enamel, stainless steel, nylon or other labour saving materials are easily kept clean by washing thoroughly after use. A glazed earthenware sink should be cleaned with scouring powder when necessary.

Special Cleaning of Sink and Surrounding Surfaces Remove all brushes and cleaning materials from hooks and shelves below the sink. Clean all surfaces surrounding the sink according to material; clean shelves, etc. below the sink. Wash the draining board according to material; where it is a removable wooden board, lift off to facilitate the cleaning of surfaces underneath it. Clean the sink, paying special attention to the overflow; clean the rubber plug with paraffin or turpentine. Clean the waste pipe by pouring down a kettle of boiling water over a handful of soda; leave to soak. Replace contents of shelves when dry. Finally rinse sink with clean cold water, adding a little disinfectant; dry with cloth well wrung-out; polish chromium fittings with soft dry cloth.

Refrigerator

A refrigerator may be kept clean by wiping out regularly with warm water. Soap, or any other cleaning agent with an odour, should never be used for the interior surface; if necessary a solution of one heaped teaspoonful of bicarbonate of soda in a quart of warm water may be used. The exterior may be cleaned with warm water and a detergent; the appearance of the cabinet may be preserved by the occasional use of a white or colourless wax polish.

Defrosting This should be done about once a week, or as soon as the frost has become ½ inch thick on the freezer. Switch off the refrigerator, or turn the control knob to "Off"; place a bowl of hot water below the freezing unit; leave the door of the cabinet and of the freezer open during defrosting. When the ice has melted throw away the water; clean the refrigerator, and dry; wash and dry containers; dry and refill the ice tray; switch on current or reset control knob; replace food.

A Cookery Store Cupboard

Remove contents of cupboard. Remove shelf coverings. Clean interior according to material; leave to dry. Clean outside surface. Attend to store jars, emptying and washing if necessary; if this is unnecessary, wipe outside of jars with a damp cloth. Clean shelf coverings where washable, or renew. Replace contents of cupboard, arranging conveniently with labels of store jars visible.

Cookery Utensils

Aluminium Care must be taken of aluminium utensils to avoid pitting or scratching of the surface. This may be caused by the use of a metal scourer, or by the use of a metal spoon or whisk, or by putting the articles away without drying. New utensils should be boiled out for 10 minutes, adding 1 teaspoonful borax to each pint of water; this prevents the formation of discoloration due to minerals in the water. Discoloration from prolonged boiling (e.g. in the bottom of a steamer) may be prevented by adding a piece of lemon to the water. Where a pan has become stained, boil with the peelings from acid fruit. After use, aluminium saucepans should be cleaned with a nylon scourer used with a fine abrasive powder or paste, or with a pad of *fine* steel wool softened with soap; frequent cleaning with steel wool is inadvisable. Rinse with clean water, and dry thoroughly. Always avoid the use of soda.

Kettles New kettles should be boiled out as above. Water should not be allowed to stand in kettles for long periods. In hard water districts, kettle "fur" should be periodically removed by a commercial removing agent.

Enamel Enamel utensils should be washed after use, if necessary using an abrasive paste or fine powder; rinse and dry thoroughly before putting away.

Roasting Tins Fill with water, add a little soda and allow to boil on the hot plate for a few minutes; empty away, wash and dry thoroughly.

Cake Tins Wipe out after use with a hot damp cloth; dry before putting away.

Frying Pans Fat should not be allowed to stand in pans from one cooking operation to another. The sticking of food to the bottom of a pan is usually caused by too much heat in cooking. Avoid plunging a hot frying pan into a bowl of water. Wash and dry the pan thoroughly before putting away.

Silicone-surfaced Frying Pans The surface is damaged by the use of a metal utensil, and therefore a wooden spatula should be used for turning or lifting food; the heat used should be less than when using an ordinary frying pan. After use, the pan should be wiped out immediately with a hot damp cloth.

Plastic Bowls and Other Equipment Wash and dry after use; do not allow washing-up bowls to become greasy.

Steel Knives Stainless steel requires no special cleaning. Ordinary steel knives must be cleaned with an abrasive to remove stains; special knife powders are available, but the most convenient agent is the abrasive powder in general use in the kitchen, used during the washing up.

Wooden Pastry Boards or other White Wood Surfaces Scrape pastry boards with the back of an old knife and wipe off all loose deposits, using a cloth wrung out in warm water. Scrub with a small quantity of soap, working the way of the grain; rinse thoroughly with moderately hot water, and finally with cold water; dry with a well wrung-out cloth. Finish drying in a current of air.

Laminated Plastic Surfaces Wipe over after use with a cloth wrung out of hot water; if this is not sufficient, wash with detergent and water; rinse and dry.

THE CARE OF CLEANING EQUIPMENT

Household Brooms and Soft Brushes

After each occasion of use, remove all loose fluff and hairs onto newspaper and burn.

Occasional Treatment Prepare warm soapy water in a bowl large enough to take the head of the brush. Clean the handle according to its material; clean the bristles by beating up and down on the surface of the water, using a cloth between the tufts; rinse in warm water;

finally rinse in cold water to give stiffening. Shake outside, and hang to dry in a current of air, with the bristles hanging downwards to drain thoroughly.

Stiff Fibre Brushes

These may be washed in tepid salt water, and rinsed in cold salt water, to prevent softening of the fibre. Brushes used for silver polishing should be soaked in cold water before washing. Brushes used for wax polishes should be soaked in warm water with detergent and afterwards washed.

Chapter 11

The Service of Meals

THERE IS SOME DANGER that, in an age when the aim of home management is to save time and labour, some of the practices which are worth preserving because they make for grace in living may be lost sight of. One of these is the attractive serving of meals. Many factors have contributed to this danger. In the majority of homes some, if not all, meals are eaten in the kitchen, where the use of laminated plastic table tops makes table linen redundant, and where the proximity of the cooking equipment suggests that serving dishes are unnecessary and only provide additional washing up. But whether the meal is eaten in a separate room or not, the habit of serving all food straight onto plates is becoming general. While it is obvious that under certain conditions the convenience of this habit will make its practice inevitable, much will be lost if the housewife does not retain interest in laying a table correctly, giving it charm and colour and often originality in decoration, even if only for special occasions. The result will give her satisfaction, and add to the enjoyment of the family partaking of the meal.

In school housecraft classes, it is frequently found that pupils, unless they are given definite teaching, have little idea of correct methods of table laying, and it is in school, especially where there is a home management flat, that appreciation of an attractive table setting may be imparted, and clear teaching given which will be of great benefit in the future. For there is no doubt that a well-laid table can stimulate appetite and aid digestion by contributing to the enjoyment of the meal; it can also convey a welcoming atmosphere to a guest. In these days of varying activities on the part of every member of a family, with hours of work and also many hours of leisure spent outside the home, the family meal is something of an occasion. It is worth making the most of it.

Some difficulty is experienced at times in explaining why certain methods of table laying are to be taken as the right methods. It can only be said that these have been handed down by tradition and accepted as correct, usually for reasons of convenience; they are useful in providing a standard to be followed. The laying of a dinner table is described in some detail, since it is the main meal of the day, and likely to be a family occasion, especially at week-ends. Some of the points stressed will apply to other meals as well.

TABLE LAYING

The Dinner Table (Fig. 42)

The room should be clean and tidy, ventilated and warm. The number to be served, and the menu, must be ascertained before laying the dinner table. Dinner cloths of plain damask are often reserved for formal occasions. When they are used, the table must be protected beneath the cloth by felt or cork mats. Place mats of linen or other material, often embroidered or colourful, look very attractive on polished tables, which must be protected by cork or other heat-proof mats placed beneath them. An individual table setting is called the cover; when deciding where each cover is to be placed, the size and shape of the table, and convenience of serving, must be taken into consideration; diners should not be crowded closely together. Place the linen in position, and a suitable table decoration.

Collect all the required cutlery, glasses, side plates and cruets on a tray or trolley. Large dinner knives and forks should be used for the meat course, fish knives and forks if fish is to be served. Cutlery should be held by the handles only, and glass and china handled carefully to avoid finger marks. Cruets should be checked to see that they are full; fresh mustard should be made if it is required. Lay each cover correctly, placing cutlery in order of courses, the first to be used to the outside; the handle ends should come about 1 inch from the edge of the table. The dessert spoon and fork may be placed across the top of the cover, the spoon above the fork, and in position to be taken up one in each hand. Large teaspoons are suitable for sweets served in individual sundae glasses. The side plate is placed to the left of the cover, with the table napkin across it; the glass at the upper right hand corner. Glasses should always be placed right way up, except in canteens where the tables must be laid some time in advance and they are turned upside down to avoid getting dusty inside. The jug of water is put onto the table just before the meal is served.

Adequate serving spoons must be provided. For a dish to be served by one person, the required serving spoons and forks, with carvers if required, are placed outside the particular cover, or on either side of the mat placed for the serving dish. Vegetables which are to be handed round should have the serving spoons placed beside the mats, or across the corner of the table. Check the table laying carefully to make sure that everything has been remembered.

The Table for Breakfast or High Tea (Fig. 43)

A coloured linen or gingham cloth is suitable. Small knives and forks are provided for the savoury course, with an additional small knife for bread or toast. Toast for breakfast is always served in a toast rack, never buttered beforehand. The cups and saucers should be placed conveniently in front of the person who is to pour out, preferably on a tray, with the necessary sugar basin, milk jug, tea basin and strainer. Handles of spoons and of china should point in the same direction to give a neater appearance to the arrangement. Tea and coffee pots should be placed to the right hand of the pourer.

A Breakfast Tray (Fig. 44)

Prepare a tray large enough to take everything required; with modern trays cloths are often unnecessary. Tea and coffee pots should be placed to the right, near to the cup and saucer. If grapefruit or cereal is served, the cooked dish should be covered to prevent cooling. The toast rack and cruet and the dishes used for butter and marmalade should be small. A tiny posy of flowers adds colour and interest, preferably in damp sand or similar packing.

Afternoon Tea (Fig. 45)

Afternoon tea is served around the fire, or with guests in easy chairs provided with occasional tables. The tea china is arranged on a trolley or low table, placed conveniently for the hostess to pour out. When there are few guests, it is often convenient to arrange tea plate, tea napkin and cup and saucer ready to be passed to each guest together; for larger numbers tea plates and napkins may be handed first. Sandwiches and cakes for afternoon tea should be small and dainty.

CLEARING AWAY AND WASHING UP

For clearing a table, the use of a trolley is convenient. After each course, remove the used dishes and plates onto the trolley, quietly and without scraping the plates until they have been taken to the kitchen. In the kitchen, remove left-over food from serving dishes onto small dishes or plates; put all scraps into the waste food bin; empty the water jug and glasses; empty the teapot, straining tea leaves and wrapping in newspaper for disposal. Stack the dishes either on the right or left of the sink; if there is only one draining board, stack them on the side opposite to it, on a working surface or on the trolley. Pile like articles together; soak the milk jugs, sauceboats, etc., in cold water and stand the cutlery in a jug or jar of hot water and detergent.

For efficient and hygienic washing up, it is essential to have a good supply of really hot water, a little detergent, a mop and dish cloth preferably of the sponge variety, a nylon scourer and clean dry tea towels. Where possible a draining rack should be used; the plastic covered varieties are convenient. The rinsing of articles is often a difficulty where space is limited. The most convenient arrangement is a double sink, or one large enough to take two square plastic bowls; where this is impossible and where there is a plentiful supply of hot water, articles may be quickly rinsed under the hot water tap. This will enable them to air dry in the draining racks without becoming streaky, and is essential for absolute cleanliness.

Wash and rinse in order of cleanliness, taking glass and silver first, and drying these at once with a clean dry towel. Continue with the cleanest china, adding more hot water as necessary for the greasy articles; finish with any cookery utensils which were not washed before the meal, drying saucepans and tins with the dish cloth. Return the clean, dry china, glass and cutlery to the trolley and put them away. Wipe the draining board, rinse and dry the washing-up bowl and sink, rinse, squeeze and hang up the mop and dish cloth. Dish cloths should be regularly boiled, and hung outside to dry as often as possible.

Chapter 12

Textiles

IN MODERN TIMES, some knowledge of textile fibres is of particular value to a housewife, for when choosing fabrics for household purposes or for clothing she is faced with a tremendous and increasing variety, each with its specific attributes. Even a moderate amount of general knowledge will be of advantage both in wise choice and in determining the laundry treatment. Broadly speaking, the manufacture of textiles entails the production of the fibre, spinning it into yarn and weaving or knitting it into fabric; the chief distinction lies in the source of the fibre itself.

THE NATURAL FIBRES

The natural fibres, cotton, linen, wool and silk, continue to be of great value and to be used for many different purposes, though silk, because of its greater cost, is less widely used.

Cotton

The cotton plant, which is bushy and 3 to 5 feet high, grows in many parts of the world, though the qualities of cotton obtained from it vary according to conditions prevailing in different regions. The plant is grown from seed; its pink-white flowers are abundant; and when they die off, capsules remain containing up to eight seeds. Each seed becomes covered with cotton fibres growing outwards, packed inside a boll or pod; the growth of the fibres causes the boll to burst and a mass of fluffy white cotton is exposed. At this stage the cotton is picked, and the fibres removed from the seeds by a process known as ginning. Here the long and short fibres are kept apart; the short ones are known as cotton lint and form a source of cellulose from which rayon fibres are made. The seeds are a source of cotton-seed oil, which has a variety of uses in the manufacture of soaps and of certain fats. The raw cotton is compressed into bales. During growth the cotton fibres are cylindrical, but after exposure to sun heat they collapse and flatten, twisting like ribbon. Their structure causes these fibres to be very strong and resistant to wear. By a process known as mercerisation, when they are immersed in caustic soda, they may be made to swell and return to their cylindrical shape. It was found that if the fibres were held stretched out while the caustic soda was washed out, they acquired lustre. In laundry treatment, cotton will stand great heat and friction, and alkali; acids may harm it, so if these are used in stain removal they should be washed out immediately. The different finishes which may be given to cotton fabrics have done much to add to their interest and variety, and to increase greatly the popularity of this material.

Linen

The linen fibre comes from the flax plant, which produces bright blue flowers, and later the seeds which are a source of linseed oil and of cattle "cake". In this case, the fibres form part of the stalks of the plant, and extend throughout its length, so the plant must be pulled up before they are extracted. When they have dried out in the sun, the seeds are easily removed; after some time of exposure to the weather, the stalks begin to disintegrate, and the linen fibres can be separated mechanically by a process known as retting. After cleaning to remove impurities, the fibres are ready to be spun into yarn. These fibres, which, like cotton, contain cellulose, are straight, not rounded, and their very smooth surface gives linen its natural lustre. In strength linen exceeds cotton, and its laundry treatment is similar. Of the two materials, linen absorbs more moisture from the air.

Wool

Of all fibres, wool has the warmest handle, and is unlikely ever to be superseded. Wherever sheep are farmed for food, wool is available, so that large quantities are produced in the world. In certain countries, such as Australia and New Zealand, farmers are concerned with the production of wool rather than of food. Wool differs from cotton or linen in that, instead of cellulose, the fibre contains a protein. The fibres are covered with overlapping scales, and are crimped and wavy; the most crimped fibres produce the highest quality of wool, which is spun into the finest yarns. After shearing, the wool on the fleece is sorted into different qualities, and cleansed before undergoing a number of processes which convert it into yarn. Two different types of fabric are made from wool: in woollens the fibres are irregularly arranged, and give a fluffy texture; in worsteds they are arranged in a parallel direction, and produce a smooth yarn. The warmth of wool in wear is due to the small pockets of air held by it, for air is a bad conductor of heat. As it is a very resilient fibre, materials made from it resist creasing; when stretched in the dry state they tend to spring back to their original length with the release of tension. Wool which is apparently dry contains at least 18 per cent moisture; it absorbs perspiration easily and in doing so becomes warmer. Although wool resists acids, it is deteriorated by alkalis, especially when used in hot solution for long periods; as it has less stability than cotton, prolonged boiling leads to decomposition. The use of friction in washing, because of the scaly nature of the fibre, causes it to felt readily. Most wool fibres shrink when first washed owing to the relaxation of stretching processes used in manufacture; on further washing, more shrinkage tends to occur, accompanied by the matting of the fibres. Because of these factors, the laundry treatment of wool must be careful.

Silk

According to traditional belief, silk, the most prized fabric, originated in China about 2500 B.C. For its production, both wild and cultivated silkworms are used; the wild silkworm produces the stronger but less uniform fibre, the cultivated produces silk of a finer quality. The carefully selected silkworms are fed on mulberry leaves and grow up to about three inches in length. When it has reached the stage of spinning a cocoon, the silkworm generates within itself a viscous substance known as fibroin; this passes through two glands near its mouth, and becomes a double thread cemented together. As it spins, the grub moves its head continuously from side to side, directing the thread into the form of an elliptical covering; up to about 4000 yards of continued double thread are spun in this way. Inside, the chrysalis forms, until finally the moth escapes from its cocoon; this is, however, allowed to happen only for the purpose of egg laying, and where this is not required the cocoon is treated to destroy life inside it. The cocoons are sorted and treated to remove the gum; they are grouped together, so that several filaments are twisted to form a thread; the yarn formed is wound into skeins. Shorter filaments are obtained from damaged cocoons, and from wild silkworms, and are used in the manufacture of spun silk. The silk fibre is very strong, soft and lustrous; it is a bad conductor of heat and therefore a warm fabric; it retains about 11 per cent moisture, less than wool but more than cotton, and absorbs moisture in wear. It is less adversely affected by alkalis than wool, and is more resistant to chemicals generally. Like wool, it is a protein fibre.

MAN-MADE FIBRES

It was the high cost of real silk, which had always been considered the most beautiful material, which caused scientists to experiment with attempts to produce a fibre which would look like it but cost less, and the earliest man-made fibre, produced in 1884, was therefore given the name artificial silk. By the 1920's the industry had become established, and it was realised that as it was much more than a cheap imitation of silk it should have a different name; the name chosen was rayon. This was fully justified, for, as the manufacture grew, a large number of fabrics with much variety in design became available, some closely resembling the finest silks, others more like linen or wool, but all made from the new fibre, either alone or in combination with natural fibres.

Rayon

The basis of rayon materials is cellulose, obtained from cotton or from wood pulp; in the case of acetate rayon the cellulose is combined with acetic acid. By various chemical processes the raw material is made into solution, forced through fine nozzles and solidified into filaments or fine threads. Manufacture proceeds in one of two ways. The first produces continuous filament yarn; here the solidified filaments are drawn together with slight twisting, the yarn varying in thickness according to the number of filaments used. By the second method the filaments are drawn together without twisting, then cut into uniform short lengths, which are combed, drawn and spun into yarn, which is called staple or spun yarn. Continuous filament yarns are used for smooth surfaced fabrics such as satin or taffeta, while the spun yarns are used mainly for fabrics with a warmer handle. Weaving by modern power looms produces diversities in the fabric, either by variations in the weave itself, or by mixing the rayon fibre with others. When self colours are required, the fabric is then immersed in dye; woven colours, as in checks and stripes, are obtained by dyeing the yarn before weaving. Fabrics are printed either by machine, which produces large quantities of material which is relatively inexpensive, or by hand, the screen printing method, producing more exclusive designs. Many different finishes are given to rayon fabrics to determine their final appearance and handle, and to meet various requirements; in some cases special effects such as lustre or crêpe are emphasised or minimised.

The most widely used process for the manufacture of rayon is the Viscose process; the resulting fabric is adaptable to many purposes and is used in the continuous filament and staple form for a wide range of fabrics and household textiles. Viscose rayon is reasonably hard wearing, dyes well and drapes well. As it is weaker when it is wet, it requires gentle laundry treatment; it should be washed frequently so that it does not become heavily soiled. It will stand a moderately hot iron.

Acetate rayon, both in continuous filament and staple form, is extensively used for different fabrics. It looks attractive and drapes very well, will take fast dyes and recovers well from creasing. The particular property of this type of rayon is its reaction to heat; very hot water should be avoided in washing the fabric, which should not be allowed to become heavily soiled; a hot iron will glaze it or even melt it.

A more robust fabric, developed from acetate rayon, is triacetate, made in filament or spun form. This is used for many dress and lingerie fabrics, and also blends well with wool, cotton or viscose rayon. The heat-setting properties of this fabric enable it to be permanently pleated. It resists creasing, shrinkage or stretching and is easily laundered, drying quickly and requiring little or no ironing; like acetate rayon, it is melted by a hot iron.

Although the manufacture of the many other man-made fibres now produced is similar to that of rayon, the raw materials used are different. Rayon is in part derived from vegetable raw materials; the fabrics which may be properly described as synthetic are made entirely chemically. Like rayon, these are moth-proof and resist mildew; each group of fabrics has other specific properties.

Nylon

The first of the synthetic materials to be manufactured was Nylon. The name was coined by the American firm which invented it, and is a term used to describe a class of materials, the synthetic fibres formed from Polyamides. The basic raw materials used are derived from coal, air and water. Nylon is extremely versatile. One of its most important textile uses is for stockings, for which its elasticity and great strength make it particularly suitable; from it are produced numerous fabrics, woven and knitted, for clothing and for household use; it is used for fur substitutes and for carpets.

In comparison with other yarns of the same dimension, nylon is very strong, and even the sheer light-weight fabrics are very hard wearing. When nylon is blended with other fabrics, it makes them tougher and more durable. Its heat-setting properties make durable pleating possible. Laundering is easy, and really hot water may be used; the fabric resists alkalis and loses no strength when wet. Having a low capacity for holding moisture, it dries quickly, and needs either no ironing, or light ironing which must be at a low temperature.

Terylene

Polyester fibre is manufactured in this country under the trade name of Terylene, and in other countries under various names. For this the basic raw materials are oils. Its properties and wide uses are very similar to those of nylon; it is particularly useful for net curtains, as it is undamaged by sunlight. It is blended with wool for skirts and suitings, and with cotton for many dress fabrics. The staple fibre is used as filling for pillows and eiderdowns, being particularly light and soft. Its resilience gives good crease recovery. Its heat-setting properties make durable pleating possible for blends of wool and terylene, or rayon and terylene. Laundering is similar to that of nylon.

Acrylic Fibres

The Acrylic fibres are also made from derivatives of oil refining and the carbonisation of coal. These fibres are used alone or blended, and have a wide variety of uses for many purposes; their softness and lightness make them particularly suitable for knitted garments, and they may be durably pleated. If laundered carefully they will keep their shape and require little pressing; if any is necessary the iron must be cool.

Some synthetic fibres are apt to become charged with electricity, which attracts dirt from the atmosphere. The resulting discoloration is difficult to remove, and frequent laundering should always be the rule for undergarments.

Man-made fibres with a protein base are used blended with others to impart warmth and softness. Other fibres have special uses for protective clothing for chemical workers, and for bathroom curtains, being chemically resistant and non-absorbent. The texture of many man-made yarns can be altered by special processes to give extra absorbency, softness and lightness. Many different trade names are used by manufacturers to describe the constantly increasing range of fabrics made from man-made fibres, and the many variations produced by special processes. Some are made in foreign countries. Reliable manufacturers use some form of labelling to show the fibre content of the material.

FABRIC FINISHES

The wide advance in textile manufacture and the production of man-made fibres has been accompanied by much research into methods of imparting new and desirable properties to textiles of all kinds. The resulting finishes which are given to fabrics have a variety of purposes. These may be to increase or impart resistance to shrinkage, to fading or to creasing; to improve the handle or draping properties of the fabric, and its appearance; to accentuate or subdue some property such as lustre which is already present; to give some new characteristic such as water-repellency. Often several of these purposes are achieved by one particular finish, the main purpose of which may be to give crease-resistance, but which also improves appearance and handle.

Because of their sources and methods of manufacture, man-made fibres are more easily altered in character than the natural fibres. In some cases, however, it is of particular advantage to be able to impart to a natural fibre such as wool a characteristic of man-made fibres, by a finishing process such as moth-proofing. In other cases it is desirable to impart warmth and absorbency, characteristic of natural fibres, to the man-made fibres. In considering all types of finish, it should be remembered that the word permanent, when used by a manufacturer, denotes that the finish will last as long as what may be considered a reasonable life for the article. Some finishings will resist six or eight launderings, after which their effects tend to weaken.

Whether a fabric is to be used for clothing or for soft furnishing, one of the most useful properties which it may have is resistance to shrinkage. Shrinkage occurs in fabrics for different reasons, of which the main ones are that the warp threads contain more crimp than the weft and tend to swell when wet; and that during the manufacturing processes the fabrics are subjected to considerable strains which stretch them, so that when the article is washed the stretch is released and shrinkage occurs. When an article is sent to a commercial laundry, the amount of shrinkage as a result of the first laundering may be considerable; when it is laundered at home by gentler methods, shrinkage may be less as a result of the first treatment, but may continue to some extent in subsequent launderings.

The finishes given to fabrics to counteract the tendency to shrink may be either mechanical or chemical. For cottons, a mechanical treatment is used which is based on the properties of elastic. While in a wet and plastic condition, the cotton fabric is clamped to the stretched face of a blanket made of some elastic material such as wool or rubber; as the elastic is released the cotton fabric contracts with it. Materials treated in this way are usually described as shrunk and are guaranteed against more than 1 or 2 per cent further shrinkage, an amount scarcely noticeable. The finished fabric has a closer texture and improved quality; the finish given is of great value for cotton overalls, which must be laundered frequently and, because of the degree of soiling, usually require methods which would be likely to cause shrinkage. Rayon, which undergoes alteration when it is wet, does not respond to mechanical treatment, and is given a chemical finish which reduces the capacity of the fibres to swell. Wool, in which some shrinkage usually occurs owing to the relaxation of the stretch imparted during manufacture, tends to shrink further by the scaly fibres becoming entangled in the washing process. A chemical finish may be given to prevent the movement of fibres without impairing the valuable properties of the wool. The resulting fabric has softer handle and is better for sensitive skins.

Finishes which impart resistance to creasing and, where desired, may be used to give glaze or sheen to the fabric depend on the application of a synthetic resin, which is caused to penetrate into the fabric; upon heating it becomes insoluble, and remains to give resistance and quick recovery from creasing. This finish improves handle and drape; it sometimes increases resistance to shrinkage, though, where necessary, a shrink-resistant process may be given in addition to it. The finished fabric takes up less water and therefore dries more quickly when washed; colours are given additional fastness and rayons additional strength, especially valuable qualities for soft furnishings. The finish is the basis of the "No-Iron" cottons and rayons, though, as many manufacturers have recognised, these are more correctly described as requiring a minimum amount of ironing, by which the majority of them are improved. Another use of the resin finish is to give permanent stiffening to lining and interlining materials and to underskirts. In the case of Trubenising, the bonding medium used is cellulose acetate, which imparts a semi-stiff finish to collars and similar parts of garments.

Another useful finish given to fabrics is flame-proofing, essential where a highly inflammable fabric such as flannelette is used for children's garments. This type of material has always been popular for inexpensive ready-made night garments, but it is very inadvisable for garments intended for children unless it has been treated by one of the flame-proof finishes.

A very useful type of finish is one which will give water-repellency; here the agent used may have a wax base, or incorporate one of the silicones. The silicone textile finishes may be given to all types of fabric, and are water-repellent and stain-resistant, though the fabrics remain porous. In addition to these properties, the drape and handle are improved and the fabric is given extra resistance to abrasion. Other finishes, such as those given by means of the crease-resisting resins, may be incorporated as well as the silicone finish. Once applied, a silicone finish will resist dry cleaning, though, to retain its proofing effect, special dry cleaning treatment may be advisable; it will resist washing, though thorough rinsing is essential.

Chapter 13

Home Laundrywork

MODERN FABRICS which are easily laundered, soapless detergents for various purposes and suitable for hard or soft water, fabric finishes which reduce the degree of soiling and the need for ironing, and modern labour-saving equipment available for each stage of the work all contribute towards making home laundrywork lighter and more enjoyable. So in spite of the convenience of public laundries and launderettes, many housewives prefer to do the bulk of the family washing at home; in small houses and flats the drying of large articles such as sheets can be a problem, and for these the use of a commercial laundry is particularly convenient. The properties of fabrics and the different detergents available have been considered elsewhere; some further knowledge of laundry agents is necessary for a housewife in order to carry out laundrywork intelligently.

GENERAL DETAILS

Hardness of Water

Hardness of water, which is caused by the presence of salts of calcium and magnesium in it in some areas, is a disadvantage for laundry purposes. Temporary hardness is that which can be removed by boiling; it is due to calcium carbonate or chalk, which although insoluble itself, combines with the carbon dioxide present in the water to form soluble calcium bicarbonate. When the water is boiled, the carbon dioxide is driven off, and the hardness, returning to its insoluble form of calcium carbonate, is deposited, in the form of kettle "fur", or scale, inside boilers. Other salts, which are not removed by boiling, cause what is known as permanent hardness. The salts of either type react with soap, forming insoluble scum or lime soap; this, together with some of the dirt particles in the washing and rinsing waters, settles on the fabric and is very difficult to remove, causing the articles to become a grey colour.

Water Softening Agents

When soap in any form is to be used, therefore, it is an advantage to soften the water, in order both to avoid this grey scum and to economise in soap, some of which will be destroyed by the hardness. Various methods of softening are possible. A commercial water softening apparatus may be fixed to the main cold water supply, so that all the water entering the house passes through the softening compound before it supplies any taps. A small portable softener may be attached to any one tap at a time. Apart from these methods, chemicals may be added to the water, and the cheapest of these is washing soda.

Soda Since any soda not used up in the softening process will remain in the water and may possibly affect harmfully the fabrics washed, or the lining of the washing machine if this is of aluminium, it is essential to know the exact amount of soda to use; a solution which is too alkaline is undesirable for a number of fabrics. Hardness is measured in degrees; the amount present in water may be ascertained from the company supplying it; 1 ounce of soda will soften 10 gallons of water of which the hardness is 15 degrees. When the soda is added, some time must be allowed for the softening to take place, varying according to the temperature of the water; at 140°F. (60°C.) the time for softening is 1 minute; at lower temperatures longer must be allowed. No soap should be added to the water until the time has elapsed, otherwise some of the soap will be destroyed. Even with commercial soap powders which are known to contain soda, this time factor makes previous softening necessary. When using synthetic detergents, however, no scum is formed in hard water and softening is unnecessary.

The most important use for washing soda is for softening water. With suitable fabrics it can be used with benefit to help in the removal of grease; extra soda may be added to a boiler for this purpose. The use of soda helps also in the removal of food stains.

Borax is a milder alkali than soda; it will not soften water sufficiently to be of much use for this purpose, since only some of the temporary hardness is found to be removed. It is used for soaking new woollens and silks, in which acid substances present may otherwise destroy soap, and for the removal of food stains.

Bleaches and Stain Removers

Sodium Hypochlorite The best known household bleach, sold under various trade names, is sodium hypochlorite, which is a strong oxidising bleach. This should be used only in a solution of recommended strength, and never on silks and woollens, which it destroys; if allowed to dry into fabrics it will cause rotting. Its chief use is for obstinate stains on white cotton and linen fabrics, which cannot be removed by milder methods; it is also a useful household disinfectant.

Sodium Perborate is an oxidising bleach used in strongly built soap powders and other detergents. Its most effective action occurs while the solution is kept boiling.

Sodium Hydrosulphite is a reducing bleach used for stripping dye from fabrics, and it acts on iron stains where an oxidising bleach is ineffective and will often fix the stain.

Hydrogen Peroxide is an oxidising bleach which may be used safely on silk and wool.

Oxalic Acid, and *Acid Potassium Oxalate* known as *Salts of Lemon*, are effective in removing iron-mould stains from any fabrics, care being necessary over the washing and rinsing of the fabric afterwards. Since these agents are very poisonous, they must be clearly labelled and used with caution; as they corrode metals, they should be applied with a bone spoon. A paste form is available.

Carbon Tetrachloride, sold under various trade names, is an effective grease solvent, particularly useful in home valeting; it is non-inflammable.

Stiffening Agents

The most usual type of laundry starch is produced from maize. Blended powdered starch contains powdered borax to give additional stiffness.

Plastic starch is available in a convenient form and gives more lasting stiffness.

EQUIPMENT

Various types of equipment, together with the new fabrics and fabric finishes, and improved detergents, all help to make each stage of laundrywork easier and less fatiguing.

Washing Machines

The cleansing principle of washing machines depends on the movement of the soiled fabrics in soapy water, and among the many different machines now manufactured two main types are used in average households. One cleanses by the action of a pulsator or turbulator, which is a disc fitted into the bottom or side of the machine and made to rotate by an electric motor. As the pulsator is driven in one direction it rapidly swirls the water and clothing around until every part is thoroughly washed. The second type cleanses by means of a central agitator which moves the water and clothing in alternate directions. Both types cleanse with excellent efficiency.

Modern machines are enclosed in cabinets made of strong stoved enamel, in attractive colours and treated against rust, and streamlined to fit in with existing kitchen units; fittings are chromium plated and controls are usually at a convenient height. Most machines are made to move easily, which is useful in the small kitchen; safety is ensured by good insulation. The type with hand-operated wringer is sometimes preferred for use in schools. Some of the smaller and less expensive machines have now, however, been fitted with electric wringers, and to these some type of safety device is fitted to ensure quick release. Often a storage compartment is provided for the wringer, and some machines may be fitted with a table-top cover to provide an additional working surface in the kitchen. Heaters, where they are fitted in washing machines, enable the temperature of the washing water to be higher than the normal domestic supply. The electrically driven washing machine which is heated by gas is particularly useful where quick boiling is required. Water is removed from the machines by automatic pumps, which operate quietly. In many machines automatic cut-out of current protects the motor from damage in the case of careless usage.

A comparatively expensive type of washing machine, used in launderettes, is fully automatic for washing, rinsing and spin drying, and is particularly labour-saving for home use where it can be afforded. Spin dryers are also incorporated in single units with washing machines and are found to be very satisfactory.

Spin Dryers

These remove water from fabrics by centrifugal force, a method used for many years in commercial laundries; many varieties are now available for home use. The spin dryer consists of a perforated drum which is made to rotate and, by the centrifugal force exerted, the water is extracted from the clothes and sent through the perforations to an outlet from the machine. With most fabrics, the time taken to extract the maximum amount of water is about four minutes; at the end of this time fabrics which do not retain moisture easily are ready for ironing, while others require varying amounts of further drying. Where the spin dryer is also fitted with a heater, these thicker fabrics are given further drying and may be ironed directly after spin drying. The safety device, by which the lifting of the lid of the spin dryer automatically stops its spinning, is essential for use in school housecraft rooms.

Other Drying Equipment

Although outdoor drying is desirable, climatic conditions and atmosphere pollution often make it unsatisfactory, and in a small house or flat indoor drying becomes a problem without some type of suitable equipment. Under certain circumstances the simple ceiling clothes-drying rack may be all that is required, but some type of heating equipment makes the drying quicker and more convenient. A light and inexpensive clothes-horse type is fitted with a heater at the base; this is well insulated and covered with a guard. Various sizes of metal cabinet, heated by gas or electricity, are available; in these the warmed air is able to circulate naturally around the wet clothing, which hangs on rails of metal or wood, and to leave through an outlet. Of particular use where space is limited is the type made of wire frame, with fabric cover, and able to fold up when not in use.

Tumbler dryers differ from the usual cabinet in containing a drum, which is motor driven and into which the wet clothes are loaded. The cabinet is fitted with a heater, often with several heat controls. As the drum revolves it tumbles the clothes through the warm air, the circulation of which is assisted by an electric fan. Automatic time controls are fitted.

Ironing Equipment

It is generally accepted that where electricity is available, electric irons tend to supersede all other types. Modern irons (Fig. 47) are light in

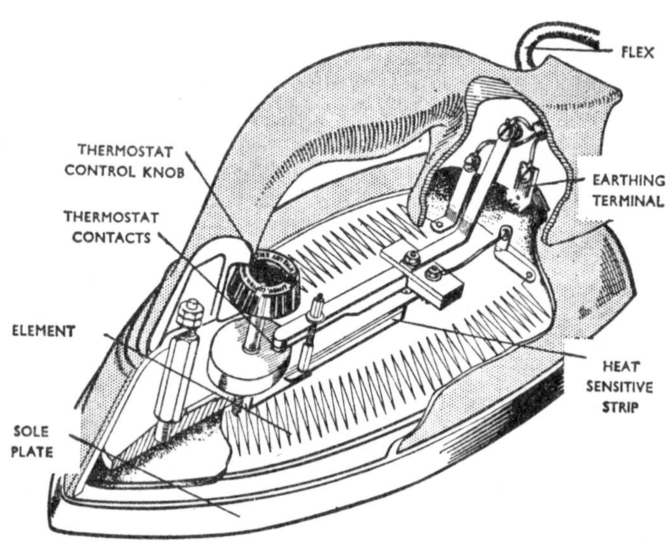

47 *An electric iron*

weight, giving good finish by heat instead of requiring much weight; these prove less tiring and quicker in use than the older, heavier type. The framework of these irons is found to break fairly easily if dropped, and special care should be exercised in housecraft classes on this account. Thermostatic control prevents overheating, and saves electricity, and is much more satisfactory than older methods, where the heat of the iron had to be tested for different fabrics.

The steam iron is now in wide use in homes. The iron is filled with water, following the maker's directions; distilled water is usually recommended, to prevent furring in hard-water districts; the water is heated and steam is forced through the vents in the sole plate. It may be claimed that fabrics to be ironed with a steam iron can be dried off completely and require no further damping. While this is found to be the case for thin unstarched cottons, rayons and other fabrics requiring to be slightly damp, starched linens usually require to be damp for ironing if a good finish is to be obtained. The steam irons are excellent for pressing woollen articles, when no additional dampness is required.

Rotary ironers and flat table pressers are now becoming more frequently used in homes. These may be operated from a sitting position and give good results from heat and pressure; the rotary ironer is particularly efficient for single flat surfaces. Since detailed work is much more efficiently finished by hand ironing, it would be unwise to depend on rotary and presser types for all ironing; their use enables large articles to be finished at home more easily.

For districts where electricity is not available, various types of gas irons are manufactured; of these the most convenient type has the heating burner on a stand; the iron is placed over the burner so that the flame heats it from the inside. Two irons are necessary, so that one may be heating while the other is in use.

Whatever the type of iron used, large flat articles are most easily ironed on tables covered with ironing blankets and sheets. In small kitchens, however, and where laminated plastic surfaces are in use for all working surfaces, it is more usual to iron on skirt boards which can be folded away when not in use; and for shaped articles, especially those made of rayon or other man-made fibres, the skirt board simplifies the ironing of single surfaces and ensures a better standard. Flex holders which may be fixed to the skirt boards keep the flex in a convenient position. The board may be covered in blanket with an outer calico cover; a smaller sleeve board is also useful. Various types of iron stands are available, the most convenient providing metal supports for the flex, which enable the flex to be wound around the iron while the iron is still hot and without danger of touching it.

THE FAMILY WASH

As in all forms of housecraft, careful planning and organisation will save time and labour. The time at which the main weekly wash is carried out will depend entirely on circumstances.

When different fabrics are to be laundered, they should be sorted into piles depending on the type of washing method and detergent to be used. Handkerchiefs should be soaked in salt water; the most hygienic method of cleansing is by boiling with a built detergent; they should be kept separate from the other articles. Tea towels should not be washed with personal articles and should always be boiled. Light woollens are best washed by hand. Stains which may be removed in the washing and boiling processes need not be given chemical treatment unless it is later seen to be necessary; iron mould and ink stains may spread to other articles upon wetting, and should be removed before the articles are put into water.

Steeping

Steep white and fast-coloured cotton and linen articles, overnight if convenient, though steeping even for half an hour will help to remove loose dirt. Avoid packing tightly; place cleanest articles on top, since the particles of dirt will fall to the bottom. Rayons, if very dirty, may be steeped for a short time in warm water with a suitable detergent. Curtains should always be steeped in warm water with a detergent for a short time. Heavily soiled household cloths and greasy articles should be steeped, after rubbing soap on the most soiled parts, in hot water with soda. Handkerchiefs should be steeped in salt water.

Cleansing

The temperature of the water, type of detergent and method used will depend on the fabric. When using soap in hard water districts, soften the washing water, and at least the first rinsing water, whether washing by hand or machine. Instructions for using a washing machine should be carefully followed; it should be filled and loaded to capacity, arranging loads according to fabric and cleanliness. Rinse all articles thoroughly, several times if necessary, until the final rinsing water is clear.

Boiling

Where a washing machine is used, less frequent boiling is necessary, since the temperature of the cleansing water may be higher than for hand washing. Boiling has a sterilising effect, helps in the removal of obstinate stains, and keeps white articles a good colour. Heat the amount of water required until it is just below boiling point; add soda to soften it and, where desirable, additional soda to act on grease and ingrained dirt. Allow a minute for the softening to take place, and add grated soap, about ⅓ ounce per gallon; when the soap has dissolved, put in the articles and boil for 20 minutes. When boiling with a soap powder or soapless detergent, follow the directions supplied. Rinse thoroughly after boiling, and wring before starching.

Starching

Boiling Water Starch Using a wooden spoon, add 1 tablespoonful of starch to 2 tablespoonfuls of cold water and mix to a smooth paste; pour on boiling water until the colour changes to a transparent grey, and keep stirring; dilute at once with an equal quantity of hot water. This is known as 1–1 starch, and is used only for small articles requiring to be very stiff. Dilute with equal quantities of cold water according to the strength required.

Examples

1–3: Aprons, overalls.
1–4: Most table linen, except table napkins which should be less stiff. Where real linen of good quality has been used, weaker starch is sufficient.
1–6: Cotton damask table napkins; good quality table linen.
1–8: Summer dresses and blouses; pillow cases.

Starch the articles requiring stiffening, and wring.

Removal of Moisture

Where a spin dryer is used, follow the directions. As a general rule, articles which if drip-dried require little or no ironing should not be put into a spin dryer.

For putting articles through a wringer, fold neatly selvedge ways and across, and put the fold in first. Care must be taken with buttons and fastenings; they may be put through rubber rollers without damage if they are arranged to one side with extra thickness of material alongside. Woollen and silk articles may be folded in a towel before wringing.

Where wringing is unsuitable, squeeze articles gently in a towel or folding cloth before hanging to dry, or hang them up without squeezing. Outdoor drying is beneficial to colour and should be used when possible. Turn articles inside out before hanging; hang with selvedges vertical; peg securely. Where a drying cabinet is used, fill from the top; fold large articles neatly and hang straight; avoid overloading the cabinet. Hang articles to be drip-dried over a bowl or bath; coat hangers are useful for dresses and blouses and should be padded with muslin for protection of the fabric. When articles to be ironed are at the right state of dampness roll them down in a folding cloth and place them in a laundry bowl until ready to iron. Cottons and linens which have dried completely should be sprinkled evenly with warm water, and rolled up tightly in a cloth or plastic bag, and left for the moisture to spread through. Where a steam iron is to be used, fine unstarched cottons and man-made fibres may be completely dry.

Finishing

Flat articles are most successfully ironed on a table, covered with a blanket and ironing sheet. In small kitchens a skirt board may be used for all articles if this is most convenient. Have at hand a wet muslin to give extra dampness to cottons and linens if necessary. Controlled irons should be set according to the fabric. Iron in the direction of the selvedge, lightly first, then more heavily, until the article is dry and no more steam arises; iron the part furthest from the worker, then the part nearest. Tea towels and other household cloths may be finished without ironing. Take them down while still slightly damp, fold and put them through the wringer several times; hang up in folds to finish drying. Air thoroughly to remove slight dampness, which although not apparent is always present after ironing.

LAUNDERING DIFFERENT FABRICS

White and Fast-Coloured Cottons and Linens

Water throughout should be as hot as the hands can bear, except for a final cold rinse. Wash by friction, rubbing strip on strip; tea towels may be spread on the draining board and scrubbed in sections with a soft laundry brush. Hard soap, or a built detergent, are suitable.

Articles with Colour which is Not Fast

Avoid soaking or washing with other articles. Use warm water with mild soapflakes or unbuilt soapless detergent, kneading and squeezing gently by hand. Rinse thoroughly several times, until no colour appears, if possible. In drying take precautions to prevent colour marking other articles.

Woollens

Loosely knitted articles which are liable to lose shape during laundering may be tacked along the seams and ribbing. Measure and record the length and width of garments and of sleeves. Steep new woollens in warm water and borax for 15 minutes, using 1½ ounces of borax per gallon of water. Wash by kneading and squeezing in warm softened water and good quality soapflakes, or in warm water with a mild soapless detergent, avoiding rubbing. If necessary, repeat washing with fresh water. Rinse in water of the same temperature, in softened water if soap has been used. Squeeze gently without twisting, and support the weight of the article when removing from the water. Fold carefully, and put through the wringer several times. Open out and compare size and shape with the original, pulling if necessary. Dry by laying knitted articles across a flat rack; heavy articles should be dried outside on a suitable day, with some wind but not in direct sunlight. Avoid great heat during the drying and airing of woollens; the heat of a drying cabinet must be carefully controlled. Woollens which require pressing may be finished on the wrong side when nearly dry with a cool iron, or when dry over a damp muslin, or with a steam iron. Air thoroughly.

Rayons

Rayon is weaker when wet and must therefore be handled carefully. Wash by kneading and squeezing, using soapflakes or mild soapless detergent; acetate rayon should be washed in warm water, viscose and triacetate will stand moderately hot water. Avoid twisting and support weight. Rinse thoroughly. Remove moisture by dabbing in a towel, or by hanging to drip; only heavy spun rayon should be put through a wringer; thin rayons may be left rolled in a towel until ready for ironing. Iron where necessary on the wrong side; the temperature of the iron must be suitable for the particular type of rayon and should be tested with care on a seam or inside part; acetate rayon must have a warm iron only. Single parts should be ironed first to prevent them from becoming too dry; use a skirt board and sleeve board, and avoid ironing over seams. Most rayons require to be evenly damp for ironing, unless a steam iron is used. Avoid damping down by sprinkling; an article which has become too dry may be rolled in a damp cloth; if this is insufficient it must be rewetted and hung out again until the right state of dampness is reached.

Nylon and Terylene

As these are strong fabrics, they may be washed in hot water, but boiling should be avoided, as it will cause permanent creasing. To retain good colour, garments should be washed frequently. Heavy articles should be dabbed in a towel before hanging out; lighter articles, and any which require no ironing, should be drip-dried. When ironing is required, the iron must be cool. Stiffened or "paper" nylon should be cleansed by moving up and down in the water without any squeezing at either the washing or rinsing stage; the article should be hung straight out of the final rinsing water to drip-dry. In garments which have lost their stiffness, it may be renewed to some extent by the use of plastic starch.

Owing to the various properties in the ever increasing number of man-made fibres, garments made from them are often supplied with directions for laundering, and these should always be followed. Where there are no special directions, gentle washing, using detergents suitable for man-made fibres and the method suitable for rayons, should be used. Knitted garments, being very liable to stretch, should always be handled carefully and dried flat. Fabrics which contain more than one fibre should be washed by a method suitable for the weaker fibre.

Fabrics treated with resin finishes for crease resistance, permanent sheen, etc. should be given gentle washing, avoiding bleach, boiling and wringing, and allowing to drip-dry.

Blankets

Soak blankets in warm water and borax—1½ ounces per gallon—for a short time. Wash in warm water with good quality soapflakes or mild detergent, pressing up and down, and using a suction cone if available, or in the washing machine, following instructions carefully, especially with regard to time. Rinse several times in clean water of the same temperature; when soap has been used, soften all waters. Squeeze gently or put through a wringer adjusted to low pressure. Dry outside on a fine breezy day, hung lengthways across the line so that the water drips from the sides. During the drying, shake lightly to bring up the pile. Where conditions make the home laundering of blankets inconvenient, it is advisable to make use of manufacturers' dry cleaning services.

STAIN REMOVAL

Stains should be treated when fresh if possible; the majority will respond to sponging with warm water unless grease is present. If possible, the nature of a stain which has dried should be ascertained and the appropriate method used. Simplest methods should always be tried first; several applications of a mild solution of chemical stain remover are less harmful than one strong solution. Bleaching should be used only as a last resort. Chemicals used for stain removing must be suitable for the particular fabric, and in the case of coloured fabric should be tested on an inside part before the stain is treated. All stain removers should be washed and rinsed out of the fabric.

Common Stains

Food Stains Soak in warm water and soda, ¼ ounce per pint. When a milder alkali is desirable, use borax instead of soda. The stain will often yield to washing after the soaking, especially where boiling with a built detergent is possible. Bleach according to fabric if necessary.

Stubborn food stains may be soaked in glycerine, after which they may yield to washing.

Iron mould Treat the stain before wetting the fabric. An oxidising bleach may fix iron-mould stain, and should not be used. Soak in a solution of oxalic acid or salts of lemon, ¼ ounce per pint of water. Effect will be more rapid if the solution is hot, which is possible for white cottons and linens; other fabrics should be treated at a lower temperature. The fabric must be washed and rinsed thoroughly after treatment.

Ink Most writing inks will yield to oxalic acid treatment to remove the iron; this may be followed by bleaching to remove the dye, where possible.

Ball-point Pens Sponge with methylated spirit.

Grass Sponge with methylated spirit.

Blood Soak in cold salt water. Remove iron mould if present. Follow by washing, and if necessary bleaching according to fabric.

Grease Sponge over clean blotting paper with carbon tetrachloride, working from the outside towards the centre of the stain.

Paint Sponge, when stain is fresh, with turpentine. Launder in the usual way.

Lipstick Treat with a grease solvent; launder in the usual way. Where the fabric can be boiled with a built detergent, the stain will usually yield.

Mildew Extensive mildew stain is difficult to remove. Where possible the fabric should be treated with an oxidising bleach, by boiling in a built detergent solution, or by treatment with sodium hypochlorite. For slight mildew stains soak in a pale solution of potassium permanganate; rinse; bleach with hydrogen peroxide, 10 volumes, in a 1–7 solution, to remove the brown stain remaining, adding acetic acid to the bleaching solution in the proportion of 1 teaspoonful per pint. Rinse thoroughly. Perspiration stains may be treated by the same method.

Scorching Severe scorch marks cannot be removed, since the fibres are damaged. Slight scorch marks should be treated at once with soap and cold water, which is sometimes effective, or by suitable bleach.

IRONING AND FOLDING

Large Plain Table Cloth While damp, fold in half with the right side inside, selvedge-ways, then take each selvedge back to meet the centre fold in a screen fold of four. Place the cloth on the table with the selvedges away from the worker, keeping it in its folds. Iron the first two sections shown in diagram; turn cloth over from left to right, still keeping the selvedges on the far side, and iron the remaining two sections. Fold by hand in a four-screen fold across (Fig. 48). Ironing by this method helps to keep the edges parallel and keeps the cloth in a convenient position for ironing, and is more easily managed by children.

Table Napkin (Fig. 49) While damp, fold selvedge-ways in a three-screen fold and pull the edges straight. Place on the table in folds, right side uppermost and top selvedge away from worker; iron in fold

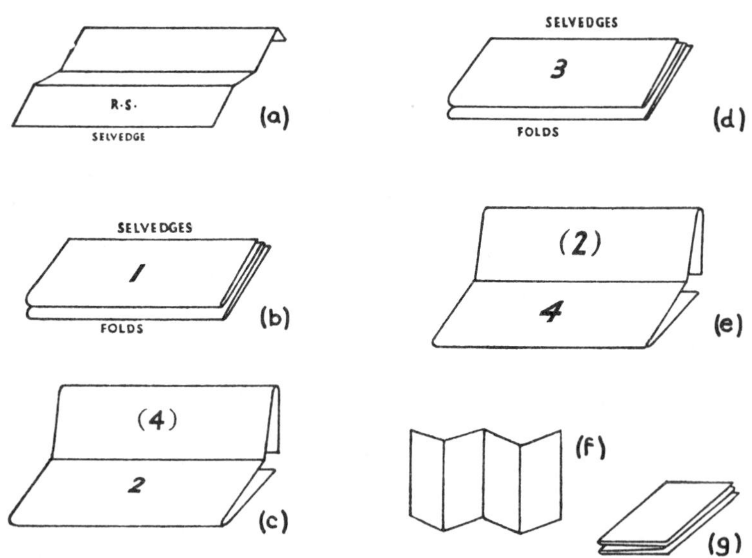

48 *The folding and order of ironing of a plain table cloth*

to set the shape, then open out and iron remaining sections. Refold, and fold by hand in a three-screen fold across.

Small Napkin (Fig. 49) Iron opened out flat with edges straight and corners square, ironing corners and edges first to set shape. Fold in four.

Tray Cloth and Table Mat Iron flat, in selvedge direction, edges and corners first. Do not fold, but store flat.

Bleached table linen is usually ironed on the right side, unbleached and coloured linen on the wrong side. Embroidery should be ironed from the wrong side, over a double layer of blanket so that it stands out well on the right side.

Huckaback Towel (Fig. 49) Iron selvedge-ways on the right or wrong side. Fold once or twice selvedge-ways according to size, then once across width.

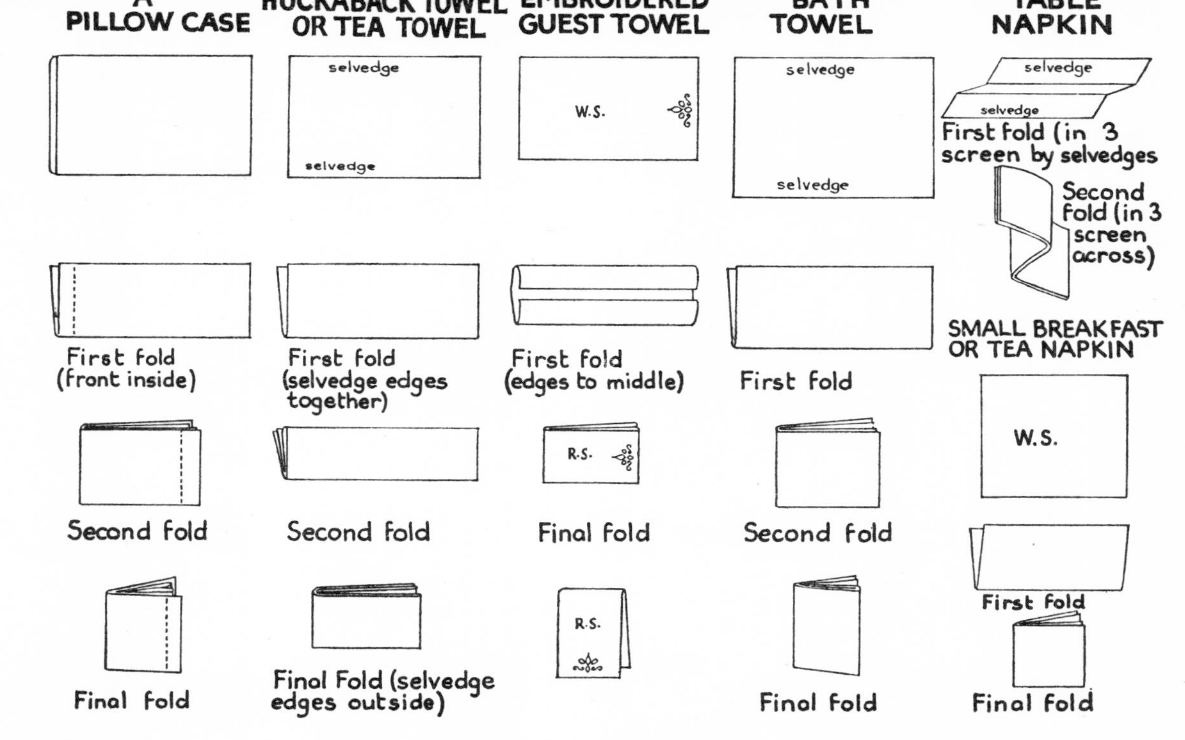

49 *The folding of various articles of household linen*

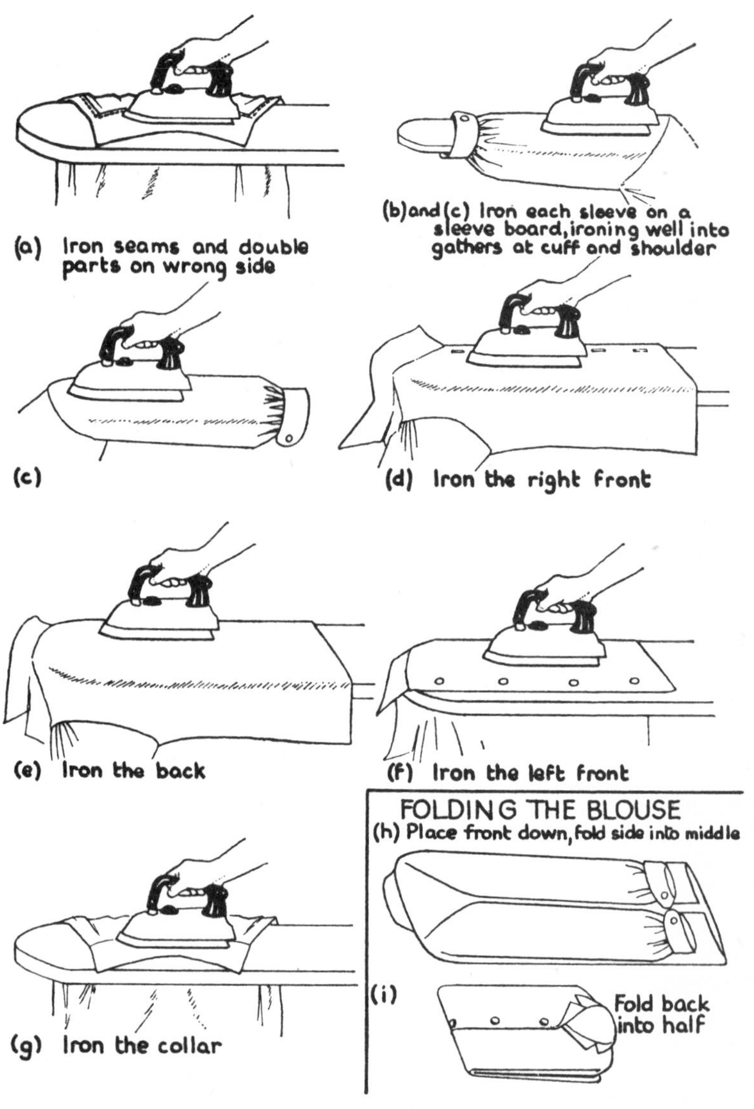

50 *Ironing and folding a cotton blouse*

Guest Towel (Fig. 49) Fold into three so that the embroidery shows to advantage, then once across width.
Handkerchief Place flat on the table, iron corners and edges to set shape, then centre. Fold in half twice, then across twice; small fancy handkerchiefs may be folded in four; initial or embroidery should show on the outside corner.
Afternoon Tea Cloth Iron opened out flat on the table. Where there is much drawn thread work it is often difficult to iron the cloth flat; in this case begin at the centre and work out towards edges of cloth. Fold in four.
Blouse (Fig. 50) For cotton blouses, iron the double parts on the wrong side first. For rayon blouses, leave the double parts until the end, since if they are treated first the single material may get too dry. Use a sleeve board. Iron cuffs and bottom of sleeve on the board, ironing well into gathers. Iron the top of the sleeve up to the shoulder; arrange finished sleeve hanging over edge of table, and iron the second sleeve. Keeping the neck of the blouse to the left hand, iron one half of the front, the back, and the other half of the front. Place the collar parallel to the edge of the table and iron last. Fasten the blouse, and hang on a coat hanger to air. To fold, place downwards on the table and fold sides into middle of back, arranging sleeves neatly straight from the shoulder; bring neck edge back to meet hem, and display with the front uppermost.

THE CARE OF OUTDOOR CLOTHING

To look well dressed does not always imply frequent and extensive expenditure on new clothes; a little time spent regularly on the care of outdoor garments and accessories will contribute much to the well-groomed appearance which most people desire, and also add to the life of the garments.

The dusty, smoky and often foggy atmosphere of town areas, with daily travelling on crowded transport, makes clothes far more soiled than they often appear, as the difference in colour after dry cleaning indicates. Frequent brushing helps to prevent this, and outer garments should preferably be brushed each time they are removed, working across from side to side. Hang outside the wardrobe for a short period to air the clothes and rid them of the smell of stale tobacco smoke which is so easily picked up in public places; never hang them where they may absorb cooking odours. Use shaped coat hangers for jackets and coats; fasten buttons and zips to help the garments to hang back into their correct shape. A suit should if possible be allowed to hang in the wardrobe for a day or two before wearing again; this gives time for the recovery of good shape, and pressing will be necessary less often. Avoid crowding the wardrobe, and keep outdoor garments apart from light dresses and blouses. Moth repellent may be hung in the wardrobe. Shoulder covers of plastic or cotton will protect coats and dresses from dust. Woollen clothing which is to be stored for any length of time should be cleaned and packed with moth repellent in plastic bags tightly sealed; it is essential to be sure that the material has not been already attacked by moth. Furs are best put into cold storage for the summer months.

Repair clothes as soon as they require it and remove spots as soon as they are made. Few things detract more from a well-groomed appearance than grease spots on clothing.

At regular intervals, valet all outdoor clothing, This is not intended to take the place of commercial dry cleaning, which is far more thorough, but it gives the occasional freshening which makes commercial cleaning necessary less frequently, and thereby saves expense. The amount of cleaning attempted will depend on how dirty the garment is.

Coats and Suits

Begin by spot-cleaning the garment with a grease solvent such as carbon tetrachloride; use a small piece of the same material as the garment, should it be available, otherwise a clean non-fluffy rag; work with the material flat on a table or ironing board, with a piece of clean blotting paper beneath the stained part. Clean with a circular movement, from the outside of the stained part inwards to the centre; this avoids an unsightly ring. Should any colouring matter remain after this treatment it may respond to sponging, preferably with distilled water. Where the whole garment is slightly soiled, working over the entire surface with grease solvent will prove beneficial; special attention should be given to the collar and cuffs. Where preferred, sponge with a suitable solution, using a non-fluffy cloth. A mild soapless detergent solution is a good cleanser; cheaper solutions may be made with vinegar and water or with ammonia and water, either of which will revive colours, though it is safer to try the effect of the ammonia and water on an inside part first. Rinse sections, as the work continues, with a cloth wrung out in clean warm water. Hang the clothing up to dry completely before pressing.

When dry, press with a steam iron, or over a damp cloth; if muslin is used, at least four thicknesses are necessary. Wherever possible, press from the wrong side; this avoids flattening the material, but is not possible where it is lined. Avoid moving the iron, but press heavily and then lift; knock the steam back into the fabric with the back of a clothes brush. For parts which have become shiny in wear, pass the iron to and fro, holding it close enough to send the steam into the fabric, but without pressing right down upon it. Ironing over pressing pads which are covered with metal on one side, used with the metal next to the fabric and damp muslin on top of the pad, often removes shine completely. Other useful aids for pressing a suit are a rolling pin, tightly covered with blanket and white cotton, for the pressing of seams, where treating them flat will cause them to mark the fabric; and

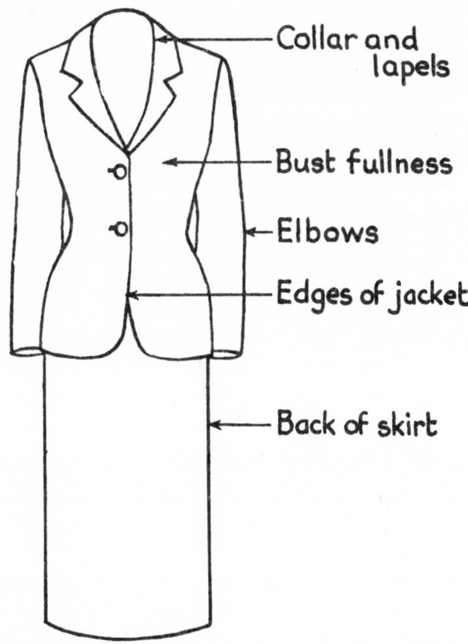

51 *Pressing a suit: parts requiring special attention*

a nine-inch square pad covered with white cotton for the pressing of shaped parts and to avoid flattening and shrinking fullness. Finally, hang up to air, and fasten buttons and zips.

Felt Hats

Remove any trimmings which are likely to respond to separate cleaning and shake in carbon tetrachloride, or treat according to material. Brush the hat thoroughly all over with a hat brush. Slip a folded strip of blotting paper inside the lining band and clean the band with carbon tetrachloride. If necessary, work over the whole hat with the solvent. Hold the hat in the steam from a kettle of boiling water, turning it round so that the steam reaches every part; steam velour from the inside. Pad the inside with soft paper and leave to dry in shape.

White Felt Hats Rub powdered magnesia into the felt all over, and leave wrapped lightly in a clean cloth for half an hour. Brush out thoroughly.

Gloves

Washable Leather Wash in warm water and soapflakes, squeezing gently and rubbing lather on soiled fingers until perfectly clean, treating on the hands if possible. After rinsing thoroughly in warm water, the gloves may be put through the rubber rollers of a wringer, fingers in first. Stretch into shape, opening fingers with glove stretchers or on the hands; dry by laying the gloves flat on a clean folding cloth or towel across a drying rack, away from heat.

Other Leather Gloves Clean by rubbing in a little leather soap with a damp rag; leave to dry without rinsing. Polish with a little white cream.

Suede Gloves Brush after wear to remove dust, using a rubber brush occasionally. Clean with carbon tetrachloride, testing carefully to see its effect on the dye. Light or medium colours may be treated with a paste of carbon tetrachloride and fuller's earth, left rolled down for half an hour, then thoroughly brushed. It is difficult to remove all traces of the white powder from dark coloured suede. Stains from leather may be removed with carbon tetrachloride, but leather dyes are often badly affected and the treatment should be given with great care.

Furs

Heat some sand on an old tin. Placing the fur on a clean cloth, rub in hot sand and roll up for half an hour. Brush well. To improve appearance, treat with a rag moistened with a little methylated spirit.

Shoes

Always keep on shoe trees or padded with newspaper to preserve shape. Have more than one pair in regular use and wear alternately. Leather soles, especially when wet, are easily damaged by heat; the steam which forms attacks and softens the leather fibres, which become hard and brittle on drying. Wet shoes should never be dried propped up in front of a fire or radiator. Stuff them with newspaper and allow to dry slowly in a current of air on their sides. New and newly repaired shoes should be worn for the first time in dry weather. The indiscriminate use of rubber soles and heels may throw the shoe out of balance; they are best applied by an expert.

To clean shoes, remove mud if necessary with the back of an old knife; remove dust with a brush; apply a little shoe cream with a rag or brush kept for the purpose, polish with a brush and finally with a soft pad.

Cleaning a Handbag

Empty the bag and brush out the inside thoroughly. Clean the lining with carbon tetrachloride. Clean the outside according to material; plastic should be sponged with a damp cloth and warm water, dried and polished with a soft cloth; leather should be cleaned as for leather gloves. Metal fastenings are usually lacquered and should never be cleaned with metal polish. Coloured shoe cream should be avoided; it is apt to rub off onto clothing.

THE CARE OF TOILET EQUIPMENT

Brush and Comb

Remove all hair onto newspaper and burn. Prepare warm soapy water with a little ammonia added; soak comb while brush is washed. Wash the brush by beating the bristles up and down in the soapy water; with some brushes, a special cleaning brush is supplied and should be used across the bristles. Rinse in clean warm water and finally in cold water. Shake, and put to dry in a current of air, preferably hanging up. Clean the comb by using the cleaning brush or a nailbrush; rinse in warm water, then in cold water, and dry with a towel.

Face Flannel

If these are thoroughly rinsed after use and squeezed out well and dried in air, they should not become slimy. Occasional boiling in softened water, without soap, will improve colour and disinfect; otherwise disinfect by steeping in cold water and any disinfectant. A slimy face flannel should be soaked alternately in solutions of vinegar and water and ammonia and water, followed by boiling.

Chapter 14

Home Safety

EACH YEAR IN GREAT BRITAIN several thousand persons are killed in accidents in and around their homes, while thousands more are injured to such an extent that hospital treatment becomes necessary, and countless others are treated at home. The seriousness of the problem has been a matter of concern for some years; fortunately, the propaganda issued by the Royal Society for the Prevention of Accidents has resulted in a gradual decrease in the number. As might be expected, many of the accidents occur to elderly people and to young children, who are susceptible to them; but the housewife, in the course of her work around the house, using a variety of labour-saving equipment and often pressed for time, is also an occasional victim.

Old houses often have features which contribute to accidents. Danger arises, especially to old people, from steps, often uneven, in unexpected places; from staircases with awkward turns, dark corners and narrow steps, and handrails in bad repair. Good lighting is essential on stairs, and steps which are difficult to see should always be painted in a contrasting colour along the edges. Falls, which account for over half the accidents, often result in an elderly person fracturing the femur. Polished floors are popular in many homes because of their good appearance; all types of wax polish will cause floors to become slippery, especially if the polishing after waxing is insufficiently well done. To overcome this difficulty, many manufacturers incorporate in their polishes an ingredient to counteract slipperiness; the polish should be described as anti-slip rather than non-slip. Polishing should not be done to floor sections to be covered with rugs. The use of small rugs on top of carpets can also be a cause of tripping and falling. The modern practice of home decorating, undertaken by many householders to save expense, sometimes involves standing on pieces of furniture to reach difficult or inaccessible corners, where excess of zeal may cause loss of footing. The untidy house is another potential danger, and children should be trained to put away toys when they have finished playing with them.

Fire in a chimney, which can very easily lead to more serious fire, may be caused by the careless use of modern solid-fuel space heaters, especially the type with doors or shutters which are closed, with the air control open, when the fire needs boosting; should the fire be forgotten and left in this condition, the chimney will most likely be set alight. The modern stove or free-standing open fire often projects rather too far forward for the existing tiled hearth, and as a result, hot cinders may fall out onto the floor in front. Many accidents, often fatal, happen as a result of fire, and could have been avoided by the use of fireguards. Electric and gas fires are now all fitted with these, but it is not possible to enforce the rule for older fires in use. Young children should not be left alone at any time with unguarded fires, nor within reach of matches. The use of flame-proofed fabric for nightwear is always advisable for children.

Electrical appliances are safe if sensibly used, and most accidents arise from lack of earthing, from neglect of necessary repairs, or from repairs done by persons who are unqualified and do not understand them. As there is danger of shock where water is present, bathroom heaters should always be fitted high, where they cannot be touched; the infra-red type, with its elements sheathed in silica, is safe. Switches controlling bathroom lights should be of the cord type, or be placed outside the door.

Where gas is used, accidents sometimes occur through neglecting loose gas taps which may easily be turned on accidentally, by failing to have leaks repaired, and by using flueless appliances for long periods without adequate ventilation.

Accidents connected with the use of oil often result from knocking heaters over, or from filling them or carrying them about while they are alight.

In the kitchen, accidents happen most frequently where there are toddlers, who are apt to pull saucepans off the cooker, or the cloth from the laid table, and who delight in picking up any sharp implement. Good training can be given to older children through housecraft lessons in school, where in crowded conditions the danger of accident is always present. Here the correct methods of using implements suitable for particular purposes cannot be over-emphasised, and much careful teaching is necessary; the arrangement of saucepan handles so that they do not project from the cooker, the training in oven management, and attention to every detail of organisation in practical lessons, where safety may be involved, will, at the same time, prevent accidents in the housecraft room and also inculcate habits which should make future homes safer.

Accidental poisoning may occur through administering medicines in inadequate light or without reading the label correctly; through leaving bottles containing dangerous drugs within reach of young children; through storing cleaning liquids in bottles which previously contained food and have not been relabelled; through inadequate care when using home permanent waving solutions; through careless spraying of insecticides.

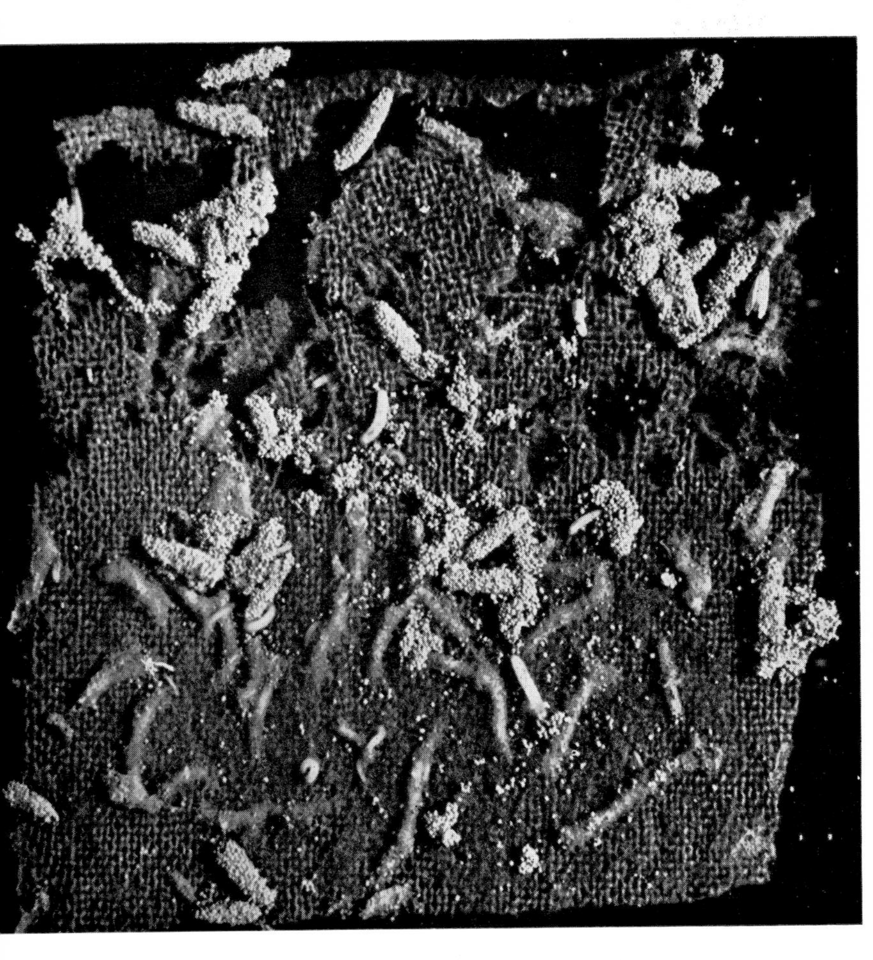

52 *Damage caused by larvae of the common clothes moth* (Tineola bisselliella)

53 *The clothes moth: egg, larva, chrysalis, moth*

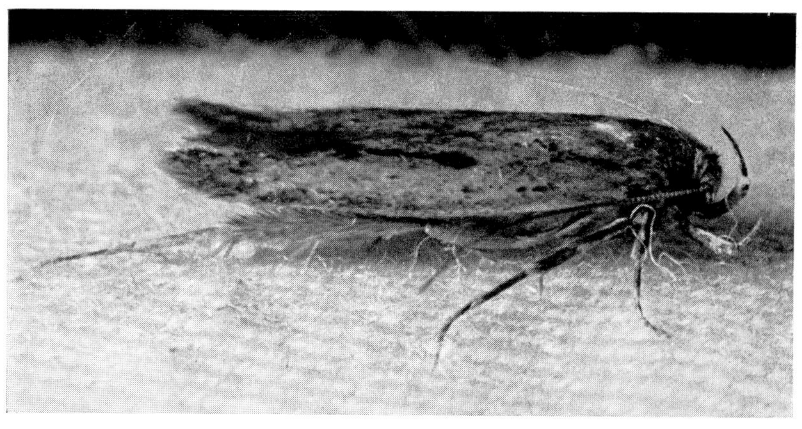

54 *The brown house moth* (Hofmannophila pseudospretella)

Chapter 15

Household Pests, Insecticides and Disinfectants

PESTS

The House Fly

The commonest household pest, and also the one which is most dangerous to health, is the house fly. Not all flies which are seen in a house in summer time are of this type; the house fly, which is grey in colour and about $\frac{1}{4}$ inch in length, has four black stripes on the middle part of its body; it takes in its food through a proboscis, which is withdrawn and invisible when not in use. In common with other pests, the fly lays its eggs in places where there will be a suitable food supply for the maggots; these include heaps of fresh manure, human faeces, and all kinds of decaying animal and vegetable matter. It is largely because of this fact that dustbins should have tightly fitting lids and no matter left exposed which is likely to attract flies. The shiny white eggs are about $\frac{1}{20}$ inch long, deposited in masses in crevices in the food material; a single fly may lay up to 150 eggs at a time and as many as 900 in one season. The rate of development varies according to the food supply, temperature and humidity, and the time from the laying of the egg to full maturity may be one to three weeks. When the eggs hatch out, the maggots grow rapidly until they are nearly half an inch in length, ivory yellow in colour; they then change into a pupa at a spot removed from where they had been feeding. The chrysalis lies inside the puparium, which changes from yellow to red, brown and finally black; the time of this stage varies from a few days to about three weeks.

Flies usually appear about June, and show increase in numbers as the summer advances. They may be seen until October and sometimes November, and a few can exist in warmth inside the house throughout the winter. It is thought most likely that the flies which breed in the following summer exist throughout the winter in the pupal form.

Since the fly feeds on faeces, and flies to its food, it can contaminate the food both by walking over it and by feeding and excreting upon it; in this way it may spread many diseases such as typhoid and dysentery. On this account both preventive measures and remedies are of extreme importance, and preventive methods should be put into operation wherever the flies are likely to breed. Many commercial insecticides are suitable for the treatment of manure heaps and refuse heaps where these are necessary; dustbins should be given regular treatment throughout the summer. Inside the house, window frames, light fittings and any other areas where the flies are seen should be sprayed with insecticides which have a residual action, the effect of which will last for some weeks. Every possible precaution should be taken over the fly-proofing of larders or any storage cupboards for food; china should be kept under cover; any food which is set out on tables in preparation for a meal should be covered.

Furniture Beetle or Woodworm

Many varieties of wood-boring beetles attack timber at various stages of its conversion; some attack it later when it is in use. The one with which the housewife most often needs to deal is the common furniture beetle. This beetle lives outside, in the dead parts of trees, in fences and gate posts, in the rafters of outbuildings; it attacks the sapwood of both hardwoods and softwoods. Inside the house it can do very great damage; it develops rapidly in damp conditions, more slowly in old dry furniture. Wicker articles and plywood are both attacked.

The beetle (Figs. 55, 56), which is $\frac{1}{10}$–$\frac{1}{5}$ inch long, reddish brown in colour, may be seen about the month of June, crawling on walls, windows or ceilings, or flying, and it lives about three weeks. Pairing takes place soon after it appears; the female lays 20 to 40 eggs, which she deposits and glues down in suitable places, in old worm holes, on the rough underside of furniture, or in any cracks in doors, floors or wood used in the structure of the house. The eggs are deposited a few at a time, and are seldom laid on a smooth polished surface; they are white and oval, just visible to the eye; about 5 per cent fail to hatch, probably owing to the dryness of the atmosphere. In four to five weeks the larvæ hatch out and begin to wander over the wood, very soon burrowing beneath its surface. As they bore, their tunnels become filled with loose dust; this consists of rejected wood and partly undigested matter excreted by the grub, and it falls out in small piles. When fully grown the larva is about $\frac{1}{4}$ inch long; as it burrows, it devours the wood with sharp hard jaws, increasing the size of the tunnel until it becomes about $\frac{1}{12}$ inch in diameter. The time during which the larva remains in the wood depends on conditions; the complete life cycle takes at least one year, but is believed to take two or more years in old dry furniture. The fully grown larva directs its way towards the surface of the wood and, making a small cell in its tunnel, remains inactive there in the form of a soft white pupa or chrysalis for two to three weeks. From this the beetle emerges, and bores its way to the outside. The exit holes vary in size but average $\frac{1}{16}$ inch in diameter. It is usually these holes, together with the heaps of fine dust beneath the furniture, which first indicate the presence of the beetles (Fig. 58).

As a preventive measure, old worm holes should be filled up with plastic wood; the application of polish, varnish or oil to unpolished or rough surfaces helps to deter the beetle from laying its eggs. Many good proprietary preparations for treating affected wood are now sold, and are very efficient; these may be painted or sprayed onto the wood, or injected into holes and any crevices on the underside or back of furniture. A suitable insecticide must be capable of penetrating the wood thoroughly, as its success depends upon this. The treatment should be repeated once or twice during the summer, and for safety again the following year. A very effective method of control is fumigation of the furniture with a poisonous gas, which will penetrate more easily than a liquid; this should always be undertaken by an expert who is equipped for the work.

The Clothes Moth

Many kinds of moths exist, but only the clothes moths and house moths do any appreciable damage to clothing and other household materials; both these varieties are exceedingly destructive, and everyone should be able to recognise them, which is not difficult.

The clothes moth (Figs. 52, 53) is a small shining golden brown moth with a wing span of about $\frac{1}{2}$ inch. Damage is done not by the moth itself but by its larvæ, and when it is known that one female moth may lay up to 200 eggs, the importance of killing every moth seen will be realised. A clothes moth observed running up a curtain or across a blanket is likely to be a female, since the weight of eggs causes it to run rather than to fly. Moths' eggs are white and oval, less than $\frac{1}{24}$ inch long, and are laid in groups of a few on any material which will supply suitable food for the larvæ. This may be woollen cloth or any woollen clothing, fur, carpets, upholstery stuffing; the eggs are laid on the surface of closely woven material or at the base of the hairs in fur; the number laid varies with different conditions of temperature, the egg-laying period being roughly about a fortnight. When hatched, the larva is about $\frac{1}{24}$ inch long, when fully grown $\frac{3}{8}$ inch and white in colour; as it begins to feed, it usually spins a thin silk tube from the fibres of the material, and feeds from inside it until the food is exhausted, when it proceeds to another patch. Sometimes the tube is left behind, and is discovered beneath a coat collar or in some similar place in clothing which has been put away. The length of the larval period varies greatly and may be over a year under some conditions; the grub can live in cocoons for long periods without food. When ready to pupate it spins a cocoon, into which it binds fragments of material not necessarily that on which it has been feeding. Within this cocoon the larva changes into a pupa or chrysalis, from which, after some weeks, the moth emerges.

The Brown House Moth (Fig. 54) Being rather larger than the common clothes moth, this species has a wing span of $\frac{2}{3}$–1 inch. Distinctive markings are three dark brown spots on the brown forewings; the moth may be seen flying mostly from May to October, both in houses and in gardens. The white larva is about $\frac{3}{4}$ inch when full grown, and is more easily seen than that of the clothes moth larva; it attacks clothing and carpets, furs and skins, collections of dried animals, birds or insects, bookbindings, leather and upholstery stuffing.

Moth Prevention Probably the most important factor to remember is that moths are particularly attracted to soiled clothing, and this includes any garments which have been worn and absorbed perspiration, even though they are not noticeably soiled. Thorough cleaning of clothing and of all articles liable to attack is therefore the most important preventive measure and should never be neglected. Woollen clothing which is to be put away for the summer months should be sent to the dry cleaners first. Blankets should be cleaned or laundered. Upholstered furniture should be regularly brushed or suction cleaned, especially in the cavity between the seat and the back and sides. Carpets should be regularly suction cleaned, especially around the edges of a fitted carpet, using the crevice tool of the suction cleaner, and underneath heavy furniture such as a piano. Curtains should be suction cleaned.

Heat is detrimental to larvæ and moths' eggs, and woollen articles should be hung out in sunshine for several hours every few weeks during the summer months, and then thoroughly brushed with a stiff brush to dislodge any eggs, especially from beneath coat collars and similar folds. Where articles are to be stored for some time, it is best to take special precautions; they may be wrapped tightly in strong paper, or several layers of newspaper, all edges or possible entry for moths being thoroughly sealed with adhesive tape. Plastic bags of various sizes, suitable for blankets, or to hang in wardrobes for coats, with zip fastenings, are excellent for storage; but it is essential to ensure that the articles are moth free before putting them in. An effective deterrent is paradichlorbenzene, and this should be sprinkled freely between folds of articles in store.

Where moths have already taken hold, baking of articles to a temperature of 140°F. will destroy all larvæ and eggs and is practicable where it is possible to do so without damaging colours and fabric.

Spraying with a good insecticide, of adequate strength, is effective if it is done thoroughly. A home fumigation treatment is to sprinkle crushed paradichlorbenzene freely into upholstery, using 2 to 3 pounds for one armchair, and cover it immediately with blankets or waterproof sheeting reaching right to the floor, leaving it covered for several days. Where more drastic treatment is considered necessary, fumigation with more poisonous gas may be carried out by an expert.

The Carpet Beetle (Fig. 57)

The carpet beetle is about $\frac{1}{8}$ inch long, oval and broad, with brown and white scales forming a pattern on its back. It may be seen between April and September. The eggs are laid on food suitable for the larva, hair and fur, wool and silk, particularly clothing which has been stored in a soiled condition in trunks or boxes or rarely disturbed cupboards, and on carpets, usually beneath furniture. The larva is brownish in colour and easily distinguishable by its hairy body; when fully grown it is about $\frac{1}{5}$ inch. Protection is similar to that against moth attack; materials are best stored in closed containers with paradichlorbenzene crystals sprinkled freely between layers, or wrapped in several layers of newspaper or brown paper with the crystals, and well sealed with gummed strips. Places where larvae are seen should be sprayed with reliable insecticide.

Silver Fish

The silver fish is a nocturnal insect, seen at times in kitchens, particularly near any source of heat, and in larders and amongst books. When fully grown it is about $\frac{1}{2}$ inch long, with a covering of shiny scales, long antennæ and three tails; it lays about 7 to 12 eggs, which hatch out in between one to eight weeks according to conditions; the newly hatched insect resembles the adult and is about $\frac{1}{12}$ inch long. The insects run very fast when disturbed, often by the turning on of a light; they eat crumbs, any starchy substance such as the paste off wallpaper, occasionally fabrics, especially those with some form of dressing. Although not a very important pest, it should be eradicated by spraying its runways with a reliable insecticide.

Cockroaches

The cockroach is often referred to as the black beetle, or in some parts of the world as the clock. To call it a beetle is not scientifically correct, for a beetle in the true sense develops from a larva or grub which it does not resemble in form, while in the case of cockroaches the young are like the adults and merely change their skins several times during the process of maturing. Two species of cockroach are found in this country, the common cockroach and the German cockroach. American and Australian cockroaches may appear occasionally in warehouses and greenhouses; they have not obtained a foothold in dwelling houses. The common cockroach was thought to have appeared in this country during the sixteenth century, probably through commerce; its origin was unknown. It spread very slowly from seaport towns inland, and has now reached most parts of the country and infected areas in all towns. The German cockroach appeared probably during the nineteenth century; it is not a native of Germany as its name implies, but probably of some part of Asia. It is given various names; in Lancashire where it appears in numbers in canteens and similar places, it is called the steam bug. It is not found so widely as the common cockroach, but where it appears, numbers are usually larger.

The common cockroach is very dark brown in colour, not black as is commonly supposed, and is just under 1 inch in length. In the male the wings are developed and the cockroach is able to fly, but in the female they are only vestiges and are not usable; there are about three times the number of females as there are males. Pairing may occur at any time of the year and the eggs are laid 10 to 14 days afterwards; these are contained inside a capsule which is about ½ inch long and ¼ inch wide, arranged in two rows of eight eggs each. The cockroach deposits the capsule in a warm sheltered place, preferably though not always close to a supply of food. Time taken to hatch out depends on the temperature and varies between a few days and some months; when ready the capsule splits in half and the young cockroaches emerge, 11 or 12 usually from one capsule, since not all the eggs mature. At this stage they are semi-transparent and pale amber in colour; colour deepens to brown during growth. The nymphs, as the young cockroaches are called, shed their skins about six times over the next four months or longer; as it nears the adult stage the nymph seeks a dark place and remains there for some weeks before the final moult occurs. In captivity the adult cockroach lives about six weeks.

The German cockroach is only about half the size, and is a light yellowish-brown colour; its egg capsule contains about 40 eggs; development to the adult stage takes about 12 weeks.

The habits of the two kinds are very similar, though the larger cockroach is less active. They like warmth and inhabit bakeries, laundries, restaurants and hotel kitchens, particularly basements, and especially where, in addition to warmth, there is damp, and a supply of food, which they find by smell. Sweetened food and beer are popular; paper or whitewash from walls, books and hair are also consumed. Having flattened bodies, cockroaches can enter easily through small cracks; preferring the dark, they shelter under radiators or behind hot pipes under cooking stoves or any equipment, under floor coverings or between the skirting board and floor, emerging at night. They do not appear to mind human beings, and are exceedingly difficult to kill owing to the speed with which they run.

These are very undesirable pests; they contaminate food with excreta and secretions from glands, and leave an unpleasant smell; they occur usually in old houses where there may be cracks and crevices, or houses in bad repair. But the modernisation of old houses often helps them to spread, and central heating helps by providing warmth and easy routes through the house. They are liable to occur in modern blocks of flats which are centrally heated, and can be exceedingly difficult to eradicate.

Methods of control should include the cementing up of all possible crevices which might harbour the pests, especially where pipes are taken through walls and flooring, and around fireplaces. A modern insecticide of the gammexane type, or D.D.T. at least 10 per cent in concentration, should be sprayed into all possible runways and likely places at intervals of a fortnight. An emulsion film, which becomes an inconspicuous coating like varnish, may be painted on woodwork and afterwards removed by washing, and will kill the pests in large numbers. Fumigation by sulphur dioxide in an airtight room is effective, but damaging to metals, fabrics and wallpaper.

Ants

Ants are social insects which live together in colonies. Outdoor ants nest in a wide variety of places, sometimes, but not always, forming mounds; the roots of plants, old tree stumps and cracks in pavements are typical nesting places. Swarms of ants on the wing may be seen during the late summer and autumn; these are flying into the air to mate. House ants nest in the fabric of buildings, and are small and not always easy to recognise; they like warmth. Ants frequently enter houses in search of food, and like sweet foods of all kinds: jam, cake, and anything containing sugar, to which they are attracted by their sense of smell.

Small infestations may be controlled by spraying all the runways with a good insecticide; very bad outbreaks may be controlled by sodium fluoride poisoning, carried out by an expert. Nests in the garden should be destroyed by pouring boiling water over them, or by treating with one of the preparations on the market produced for that purpose.

Mosquitoes

Although in this country the danger of disease by mosquitoes does not exist, they can be a troublesome pest especially where houses are built near a river or lake. Mosquito eggs are black, about $\frac{1}{24}$ inch in size, and are usually laid on water, glued together. The larval period is passed in the water, the grubs feeding on animal and vegetable matter, and coming to the surface to breathe. After a period of growth varying from a few days to several months, the larva goes into a pupa state, from which the mosquito emerges in a few days. There are in this country 32 different types of mosquito, with different habits; some do not bite human beings at all, others bite more freely in the house than in the open. Some species are most troublesome in spring, others in autumn.

To control these pests, rain-water barrels or other containers should be kept covered, and any pools or known breeding places sprayed at the right time of year according to the species; specimens may be identified at a natural history museum. Inside the house any good insecticide sprayed on walls will usually prove efficient, destroying by contact in a few minutes. To prevent mosquito bites a cold cream containing dimethyl-phthalate may be rubbed into the skin; this repels on contact and gives protection for several hours. Other antiseptic lotions or creams are usual for application after bites.

INSECTICIDES

Many of the insecticides now available are based on benzene hexachloride. These are known as "Gammexane" insecticides; they are manufactured in different forms and are available for both indoor and outdoor uses. Fine powders of this type have no residual odour, are effective against a wide range of household pests including cockroaches, flies and silver fish, and continue to kill them for a long period if left undisturbed around skirting boards and in similar places. These powders do not injure fabrics and may be used as a protection against moths and carpet beetles, only a light film of dust being required. Gammexane emulsions, which may be diluted with either water or oil, are intended to be used for spraying walls and similar surfaces, and give a film which lasts for many weeks. Where water is used to dilute the emulsion, there is no fire risk; the spray must not be allowed to come into contact with foodstuffs. Where it is desirable to make the effect of the spray more rapid, pyrethrum or any other rapidly killing insecticide may be added. For knocking down and killing flying insects, the concentrate is added to odourless kerosene containing pyrethrum, and the mist sprayed through fine nozzles; although this does not give

55, 56 *The common furniture beetle* (Anobium punctatum)

57 *The varied carpet beetle* (Anthrenus verbasci)

58 *A chair damaged by the common furniture beetle*

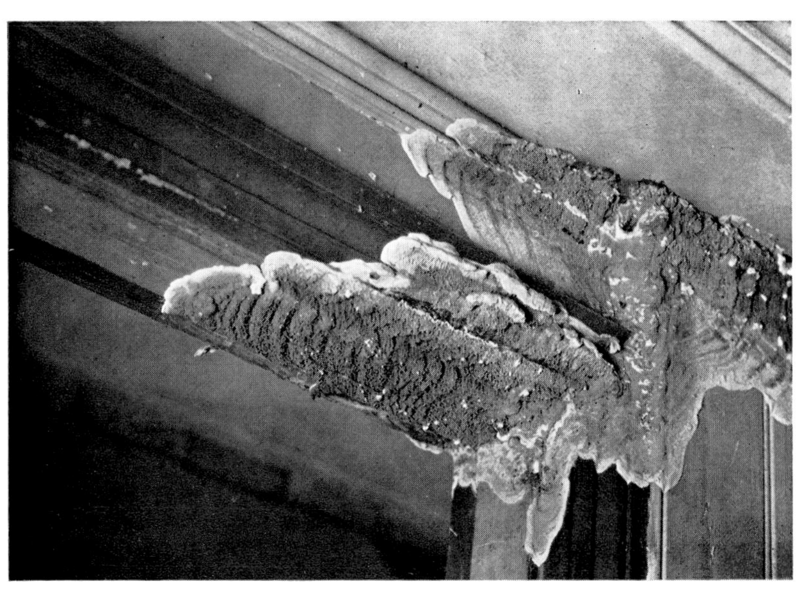

59 *Damage by dry rot at the top of a doorway*

a lasting effect owing to its dilution, it quickly clears flies and mosquitoes at the time of use.

Gammexane is also incorporated into a smoke-generated mixture; when the generators are ignited, the smoke settles on surfaces and leaves a thin film which remains active for some weeks; the generators are often used where oil sprays are undesirable because of fire risk. The room to be treated should first be emptied of all foods, cookery utensils and dyed silk or rayon fabrics which might become discoloured; all openings into the room should be closed or blocked up. After lighting the generators, the size and number of which will depend on the size of the room, they should be left for at least two hours.

Many of the insecticides containing D.D.T., often combined with pyrethrum, are available in both powder and liquid form, and are suitable for many varieties of pests; where the concentration of D.D.T. is sufficiently high, they are effective and lasting. The best have a concentration of 10 to 20 per cent.

DISINFECTANTS

It is desirable in a disinfectant for use in the home that it should have a high activity against a variety of bacteria, be pleasant to use and not irritating to the skin. The antiseptic Chlorhexidrine fulfils these conditions; it is intended mainly as a preventive measure against infection and has been produced in different forms for various circumstances. The liquid antiseptic has many uses in first aid, in the sickroom and for general household purposes; as a cream it is pleasant to use and harmless to the skin; lozenges into which it is incorporated are effective both in prevention and treatment of throat infections, the addition of other ingredients helping to give relief from pain and irritation. Cetrimide is now a well-known antiseptic which can destroy all the bacteria likely to be encountered on the skin. It is a detergent as well as a bactericide, and is used to clean and disinfect in one operation. Solutions are colourless and odourless, and do not deteriorate on keeping; when incorporated into a cream it has no harmful effect, does not cause pain or irritation, is readily absorbed and does not make the skin greasy or sticky. A modern liquid antiseptic which contains both these bactericides, Chlorhexidrine and Cetrimide, is now produced and is suitable for home and school use.

BARRIER CREAMS

Barrier creams are extremely useful for protecting the hands from the effect of housework; some varieties are equally good for wet or dry work. These prevent soreness and irritation arising from the use of strong detergents and other cleaning agents, and give protection during paint cleaning, car cleaning or any other heavy work, providing an effective barrier against dirt and grime and a safeguard against dermatitis.

Chapter 16

Soft Furnishings

CHOICE OF SOFT-FURNISHING FABRICS

Faced as she is with such a large number of fabrics from which to choose, an experienced housewife selecting materials for soft-furnishing purposes needs some broad principles of guidance. In the majority of households the fabrics are intended to last for some years, and may be expected to withstand both winter fogs and summer sunshine; the atmosphere of town areas is likely to have a more deleterious effect than that of country districts. For most uses, therefore, cheap fabrics are inadvisable, and to buy the best that can be afforded is always a good rule. Both natural and man-made fibres are made into fabrics which are suitable for soft furnishing; often these are blended from two or more fibres. It is therefore wise to find out exactly which fibres are present, and to consider their specific properties and how these will affect the wearing qualities under the conditions in question. The fabric must stand up well to washing or dry cleaning. Both for curtains and for loose covers, shrinkage is of particular importance. Here the modern shrink-resistant finishes given to soft-furnishing fabrics are well worth their extra cost.

It should be remembered that design includes colour, pattern and texture, and that all of these must be considered. Whether it is for curtains or for loose covers, the fabric must blend in well with the remaining decoration and furnishing of the room for which it is intended; it should fit in with the character of the room, which may be formal or otherwise. Much material giving useful advice on colour schemes, and charts showing different combinations of colour, are available to the housewife. Both natural and artificial lighting should be taken into account, and pale colours avoided in dark, north rooms, where clear bold colours are usually preferable. It is a great advantage when colours are guaranteed to be fast to washing and in sunlight. As a general rule, some contrast in colour and in pattern between the big items in the room is pleasing; too much pattern leads to confusion and should be avoided. Where pattern is present, its size should be in scale with the size of the room and of the furniture; large rooms with big windows can take large, bold patterns, which would make a small room appear smaller by standing out too much. Where, however, the repeat of pattern is large but the pattern contains small scale detail, it may often be used in a small room satisfactorily; when viewed from a distance, small patterns are often lost. Patterns which are printed merely on the surface of the fabric are to be avoided. Contrasts in texture in a room are pleasing where they are wisely chosen, but must be considered in relation to the style of the room. Chintz and velvet look well together; a glossy rayon bedspread will be unsuitable with coarse crash curtains.

Where the fabric chosen is to be used for curtaining, special consideration should be given to its draping qualities, and it should always be viewed draped rather than in a roll. Whether the curtains are to be lined or unlined will have some influence on the choice of fabric. Lined curtains hang better, and keep out draughts more successfully; their colours and patterns will show more distinctly. Many people prefer the uniform appearance to the outside of the house obtained by lining all curtains. Unlined curtains have the effect of reducing the colour.

For loose covers, the texture is important; a close, firm weave is always harder wearing, and keeps dust from the upholstery beneath it. The material chosen must not crease easily; it should not shrink. Pattern will stand out more clearly on a chair than when draped; for covers the repeat of pattern should be reasonably small; very large patterns always lead to wastage in cutting. Loose covers are intended to protect the upholstery from soiling and from wear; they should be easily washed or cleaned, and if washable should withstand fairly vigorous treatment.

Glass or net curtains are chosen where they are essential for privacy, or where it is an advantage to hide the bare, hard appearance of window frames; in some rooms they help to give a dainty appearance; in others it may be desirable to subdue bright sunlight. For these, synthetic fabrics give the longest wear.

MAKING OF CURTAINS

Measurements

Measure the length, from the curtain rail to the point where the curtain will finish. Short curtains may be made to reach the window sill, or where this is sufficiently narrow, to hang about 6 inches below it; long curtains should hang to a point ½ inch from the floor. Add 6 inches for the heading and hems, and extra for patterned material, according to the repeat of pattern. Measure the width of the window; the curtaining material should be sufficient to cover at least one and a half times this measurement. Calculate the number of widths of material necessary for this, allowing an extra 3 inches on each curtain which will be taken up by the side hems. Material required: multiply the length calculated by the number of widths of fabric required for the whole window.

Patterned Material

The curtains must be cut so that the pattern in each will correspond. If more than one width of material is required for each curtain, join with flat seams at opposite sides, matching the pattern.

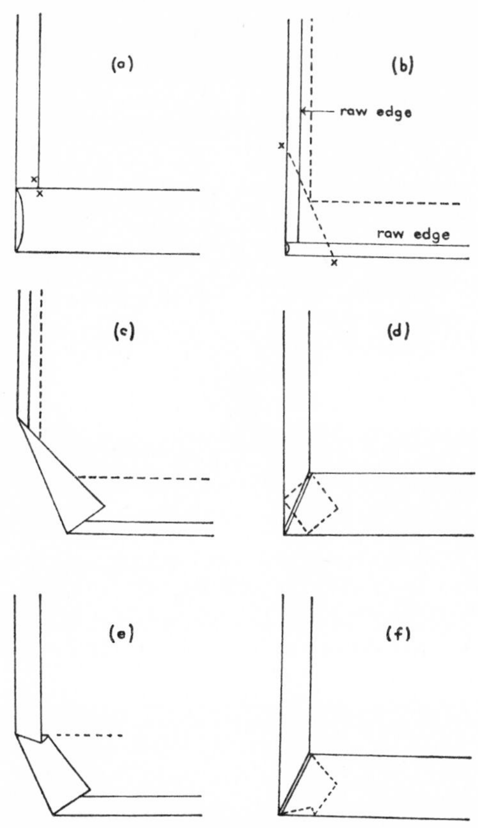

60 *A mitred corner: note that* (e) *and* (f) *are alternatives to* (c) *and* (d)

Unlined Curtain (Fig. 60)

Remove selvedges, or snip at intervals; make a 1-inch hem at each side, and at least 3 inches at the bottom. Mitre the corners neatly. Fold

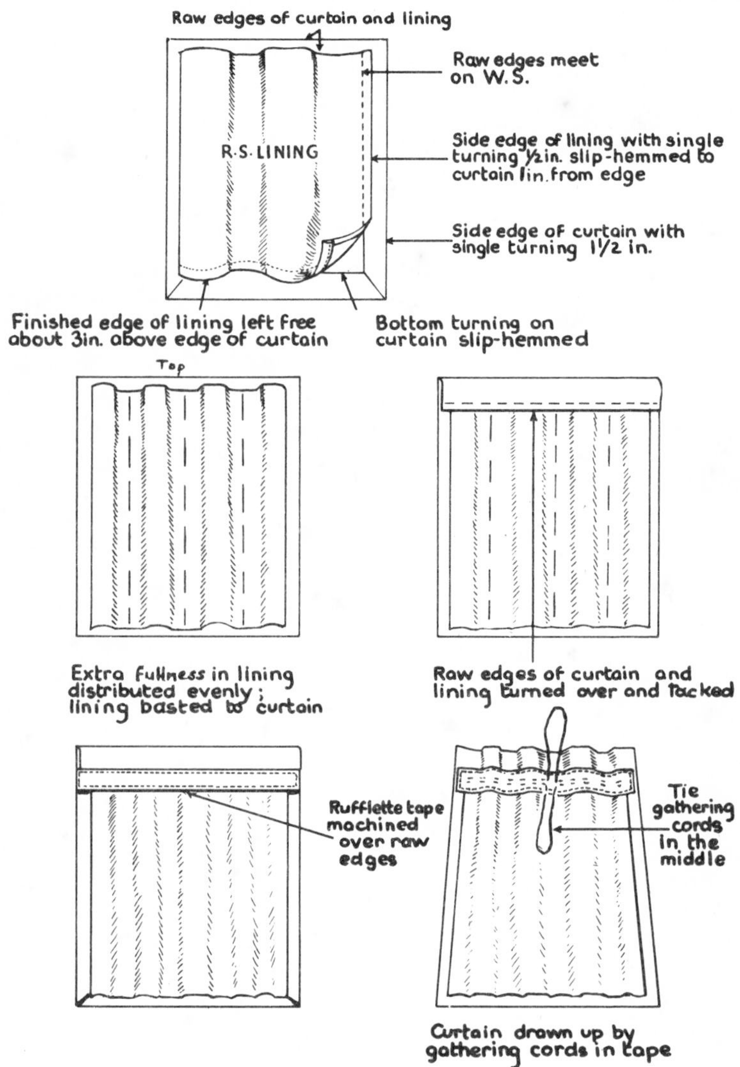
Raw edges of curtain and lining
Raw edges meet on W.S.
R.S. LINING
Side edge of lining with single turning ½in. slip-hemmed to curtain 1in. from edge
Side edge of curtain with single turning 1½ in.
Finished edge of lining left free about 3in. above edge of curtain
Bottom turning on curtain slip-hemmed
Top
Extra fullness in lining distributed evenly; lining basted to curtain
Raw edges of curtain and lining turned over and tacked
Rufflette tape machined over raw edges
Tie gathering cords in the middle
Curtain drawn up by gathering cords in tape

down a single turning at the top of the curtain, the width of the heading required; 1½ inches will be sufficient where the curtains are to hang below a pelmet or pelmet board. If no pelmet is used, a wider turning is necessary to conceal curtain fittings; tack down. Place Rufflette tape over the raw edge, turning under its ends, tack and machine along top and bottom edges and ends of tape. Slip hooks into the tape at intervals of 4 inches. Draw up the gathering cords of the tape at the middle and tie.

Lined Curtain (Fig. 61)

Cut out the curtain and lining. With most fabrics, it is an advantage to allow plenty of ease in the lining, which may be cut the same size as the curtain material; where it is preferred to have less ease, the lining may be made slightly smaller. On the side edges of the curtain make single turnings of 1½ inches and tack. Finish the bottom edge with 3 inches turning as above, and slip hem by hand. On the lining, tack single ½-inch turnings on the side edges, and finish the bottom edge with a 1-inch hem, which may be machined. Place the wrong side of the lining to the wrong side of the curtain, the side edges of lining 1 inch from the edge of the curtain, the lower edge of the lining about 3 inches up from the bottom of the curtain. Tack and slip hem the side edges of lining to curtain; leave the bottom free. Ease the lining very slightly as the side edges are joined. Distribute the extra width in the lining evenly and baste the lining to the curtain all down the length, at the centre and quarter marks; this assists the lining and curtain to hang well. Turn over the curtain material and lining at the top, trimming off superfluous lining, and finish by covering the raw edges with Rufflette tape as for unlined curtains. Remove basting.

It is always preferable to make most of the curtain by hand rather than by machine. With certain materials, however, where shrinkage is not expected, and where materials are suitable, the curtains may be made entirely by machine. In this case, finish the bottom hems of curtain and lining. Place lining on the curtain, right sides together, lower edges arranged as above; tack side edges together ½ inch from the raw edge and machine. Turn to right side; arrange position of the seam 1 inch from the curtain edge; finish the curtain as above.

MAKING OF LOOSE COVERS

Certain general points should be remembered in making all types of loose cover. The turning allowance should be at least 1 inch on all seams; the cover must fit sufficiently loosely to allow it to be taken on and off easily; extra allowance for possible shrinkage is advisable unless

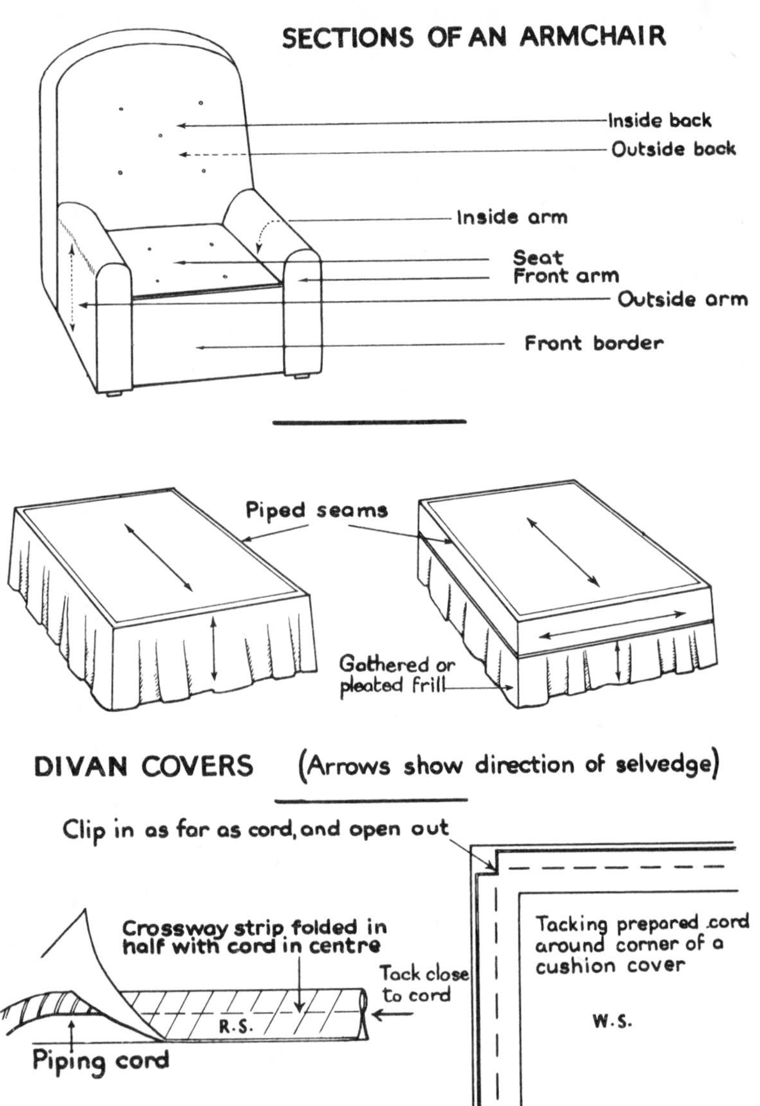

62 *Loose covers: sections of a armchair; divan covers; piping the seams*

the material is known not to shrink. The piping of conspicuous seams adds a neat appearance to most covers. For this, piping cord is obtainable in different thicknesses, the choice depending on the fineness or otherwise of the covering fabric. If it is not pre-shrunk the cord should be boiled for five minutes before use to prevent the subsequent puckering after the covers have been washed.

Preparation of the Piping Cord (Fig. 62)

Wherever this must be taken around a curve, it must be covered with crossway strips. For straight edges, strips cut to the straight thread may be used, though in patterned fabrics the effect of the piping is improved by the use of cross-way material; for cushion covers, its use will improve the appearance of corners. Cut the strips the width required according to the thickness of the cord and the turning allowance. Join into one long length sufficient for all the piping; placing the cord in the centre, on the wrong side, fold the strip in half right side out and tack close to the cord. Place the prepared piping cord along one of the edges to be joined, on the right side, raw edges together, and tack close to the cord; place the second edge on top, right sides together, raw edges together, and tack close to the cord. Machine on the wrong side through all thicknesses, using a piping foot.

A Cushion Cover

Cut out the cover, allowing turnings but making the finished cover ½ to 1 inch smaller than the cushion pad on all sides. Beginning away from a corner, tack the prepared piping cord around the four edges; the ends of the cord should meet and be held together by twisting cotton around them; the ends of the covering strip should be joined along the straight thread. To make a neat corner, clip in as far as the cord and open the cut edges to make a right angle. Attach the second half of the cover, leaving an opening, and finish by machining. Trim raw edges and clip away the corners of the cushion cover to ensure neatness when it is turned to the outside. Finish the opening with a placket and fastenings, and neaten all raw edges.

A Divan Cover (Fig. 62)

This may be made with a deep flounce attached to the top section, or with a box edge between the top section and the frill. Measurements should be taken over the bedding. Selvedge threads should run down the length of the bed in the top section, parallel to the long seams in box edges, and down the depth of the flounce or frill. The flounce may be gathered or pleated; for gathers allow at least one and a half times the finished length; for fine materials, twice the finished length gives a fuller effect. Where the divan cover is intended to fit over pillows, a gusset inserted between the top section and the flounce will enable the gathers to hang evenly to the floor. Seams may be piped.

An Armchair Cover

Since armchairs are made in a variety of shapes, general directions must be adapted to the particular type of chair. The simplicity of design in modern chairs removes many of the difficulties from the cutting and making-up of loose covers. To calculate the amount of material required, divide the chair into sections (Fig. 62), and measure the length and width of each, taking length measurements from the highest point of the section, and width measurements across its widest part. In the older conventional armchair, the sections will be the inside back, the outside back, the seat, the inside arms, the outside arms, the front arm pieces and the front border. Where a tuck-in is necessary, allow 4 to 6 inches extra for it on the inside back and inside arms, and on the corresponding back and sides of the seat.

Plan carefully, by means of a rough sketch, how each piece to be cut will fit onto the material, bearing in mind its width and pattern, the main features of which must appear at the centre of the inside back and seat. Inside arms pieces should match. Except in the case of a frill, selvedge threads should run to length measurements.

To cut and make the cover, place the material on the chair, and mark round the shape of each section in turn with chalk; cut out each, allowing for adequate turnings. Cut two pieces together for both inside arms. Beginning with the seat and inside back, tack the sections together in position on the chair, with the wrong side outwards, fitting carefully and inserting darts where the shaping requires them. When joining the outside back section, leave an opening from its widest point to the floor. Remove the cover carefully, insert piping cord in the seams where required, and machine. Finish the opening with a placket and fastenings. Neaten all raw edges.

SIMPLE HOME UPHOLSTERY

A knowledge of upholstery is invaluable since it enables repairs to furniture to be done at home at the minimum expense. Modern materials have simplified the work, and few tools are necessary; the use of a web strainer, of which several different types are available, is advised when webbing a chair seat, for it is difficult to pull the webbing as tight as it should be without it.

Pincushion Upholstery for a Chair or Stool (Fig. 63)

Where the frame has been previously upholstered, remove all old tacks, loosening them with a hammer and old screwdriver. Strip off all old covering material and stuffing. If necessary, rub down the frame and re-stain it.

Materials Required Upholsterer's webbing, 2 inches wide, sufficient to fix strips in both directions across the frame, about 1 inch apart. Tacks, $\frac{1}{2}$ inch and $\frac{3}{8}$ inch. Hessian, outer covering material, stuffing of cotton flock, etc., gimp and suitable adhesive.

Carefully mark with a pencil on the top rail the position of the strips of webbing. Although in heavier work $\frac{5}{8}$ inch improved tacks are used for fixing the webbing, the rails of a small stool or occasional chair are usually too slender to take these without splitting, and ordinary $\frac{1}{2}$ inch tacks may be used. Beginning at the centre strip, fold back 1 inch at the end of the webbing and fix it with 3 to 5 tacks on the top of the rail, $\frac{1}{4}$ inch from outer edge. Using a web strainer, pull the webbing to the opposite side, straining it as tightly as possible; this should be repeated until it will not stretch any more. Still holding it firmly, drive in three tacks; cut off the webbing about 1 inch from them, fold over the end and fix with two more tacks. Repeat with the remaining strips in the same direction as the first. Then, beginning with the centre again, fix the cross strips, interlacing them. Cover the webbing with a piece of hessian, the size of the frame with 1 inch turnings; turn in the edges, and tack on top of the frame, working from the centre out to the corners and using $\frac{3}{8}$-inch tacks; pull it taut. Using a curved needle and twine, stitch "bridle" loops about 4 inches long around the edge and about 1 inch from it, leaving each loop loose enough to slip a hand beneath it. Tease out each handful of stuffing; stuff it under the loops to make a tightly packed roll which will help to keep the stuffing in place. Evenly pack the centre hollow until there are no thin places and the stuffing forms a curve. Cut hessian large enough to cover it; this should have 1-inch turnings and may be taken down over the sides of the stool frame to the depth preferred. Tack from the centre out to the corners along one edge, using temporary tacks which may be easily removed; pull the hessian firmly over the stuffing and tack at the opposite side in the same way, then adjust tacks until the material is sufficiently taut. Repeat at the remaining two sides. See that the folds of the hessian are on a straight thread along parallel sides. Special care must be taken to neaten the corners, adding additional stuffing if necessary to procure a good shape, and cutting away superfluous material to avoid bulk. Knock all tacks home. Fix the outer covering material in the same way, tacking it just below the hessian. Finish by covering the edges with suitable gimp or braid; this may be fixed with a

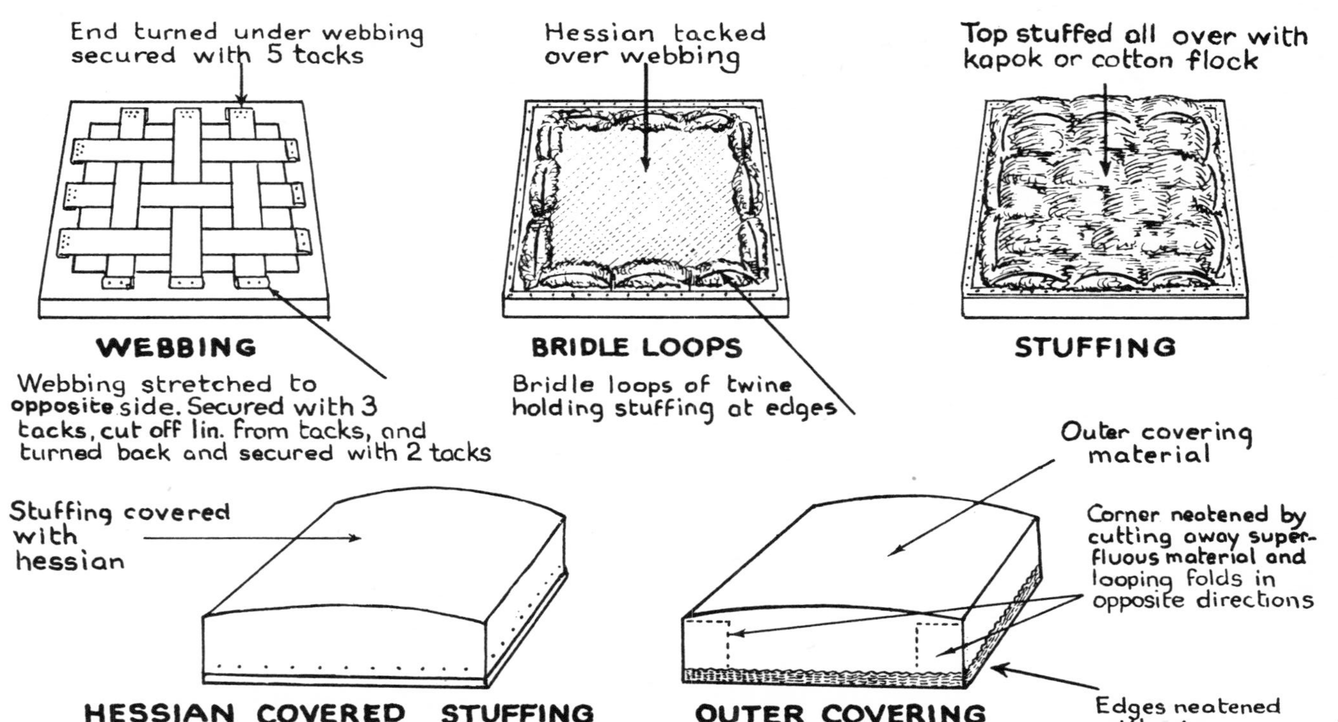

63 *Upholstering a stool top or chair seat*

suitable adhesive, joining it neatly at one corner. Turn the stool or chair upside down and tack a piece of glazed linen or hessian on the bottom, taking it to within ¼ inch of the outer edge of the rail and carefully shaping it around the legs.

Latex Foam Upholstery

This may be used on top of webbing, or on a solid wood or plywood base; in the latter case, drive several small holes in the wood to provide ventilation. The latex foam may be applied in two ways, according to its thickness and solidity.

1. *Squared Edges* Cut the latex foam the same size as the stool frame, using a ball-point pen to mark the cutting edge, and saw-edged scissors for cutting. Cut strips of calico 2 inches wider than the depth of the rubber, and with a rubber adhesive stick 1 inch of calico around the edges of the rubber; dust with french chalk. When firmly stuck, place the rubber in position on the top of the stool; draw the strips down to the side edges of the frame, firmly but not sufficiently tight to pull the rubber into ridges, and tack to the frame. The top cover may then be fixed in the usual way.

2. *Feathered Edges* For these the latex foam should be cut larger than the frame by ½ inch on each side. Taper the edge of the rubber on the cavity side to an angle of 45 degrees. Cut 2-inch strips of calico, stick to the edges of the rubber, and dust with french chalk; pull the strips down until the edge of the rubber meets the edge of the rail, and tack to the sides. Fix the top cover, pleating it carefully at the corners to obtain a neat rounded shape. Finish with gimp or braid.

Chapter 17

Household and Electrical Repairs

REPAIRING FLOOR COVERS

Carpets

The production of good household adhesives which effect lasting repairs to carpets and are quickly and easily applied has caused the more laborious methods to be largely superseded and has made it possible to cut and fit carpeting without difficulty. For valuable carpets and where great strength is required the methods of finishing edges and of joining by stitching may be preferred.

Carpet Edge Cut a piece of carpet binding the length of the edge and with sufficient for two small single turnings at each end; apply adhesive and stick down the turnings. Trim the edge of the carpet straight by cutting along a thread; apply the adhesive according to directions, usually to binding and back of carpet. When tacky, apply the binding to the carpet back, bending the edge of the binding so that it comes up to the top of the pile; this helps to prevent fraying at the edge. Hammer into position to exclude air and ensure a firm flat finish. For a loosely woven carpet which is likely to fray, first remove the pile for about half an inch from the edge, fold back the edge and stick down with adhesive; cover with binding. Alternatively, adhesive binding is available in various widths and may be applied with a hot iron.

Joining Carpet Taking a piece of binding the length of the join, crease down the centre lengthways and with suitable adhesive stick one edge to be joined so that it reaches the crease; apply the second edge to meet the first, matching the pattern carefully.

Stitched method for edges and joins, suitable for edges at right angles to the cotton warp threads:—Remove the pile and weft threads for ¾ inch; divide threads into groups of six or eight, twist together, and backstitch the bundles onto the carpet backing with two rows of stitching, one close to the edge and the other ¼ inch below the first; use a carpet needle and carpet thread. To join, prepare both edges in this way, then join by an oversewing seam, taking care to avoid a ridge.

Patching a Carpet This repair is sometimes made necessary by a burn from a cinder or cigarette. Remove the damaged part by cutting around it along the straight threads of the backing. Cut a patch to fit exactly, matching the pattern. Prepare a square of hessian larger than the hole and stick it firmly with adhesive to the back of the carpet over the hole. Apply adhesive to the patch, and when tacky carefully insert it and stick it to the hessian. In joining or patching carpets, care must be taken to see that the pile on both pieces is running in the same direction, otherwise the repair will be unnecessarily conspicuous.

Linoleum Repair

Using a linoleum knife and safety ruler, cut a square or oblong piece of linoleum to cover the worn part, matching the pattern carefully. Using the patch as a guide, cut away the worn part so that the patch fits exactly into the hole. Insert it and fix with linoleum brads about 1½ inches apart and fixed alternately on either edge about ¼ inch from the join; see that there is a brad in each corner of the patch. If preferred, the patch may be fixed with adhesive to the floor.

ELECTRICAL REPAIRS

These should be attempted by somebody fully understanding them and only the simple ones should be undertaken by a householder.

Mending a Fuse

If a faulty appliance is known to have caused the fuse to blow, remove it. Switch off the main supply of current; in many fuse boxes the handle works the switch and the box can be opened only by disconnecting the current. Examine the fuse holders in order to discover which one has been affected; if the break is not obvious, pull the wires gently until it has been located. Remove the old fuse wire, and replace by winding the end of the new wire round one terminal in a clockwise direction and guiding the other end along the groove or through the tunnel in the porcelain and securing it to the other terminal; avoid using too tight a wire as this may soon break again. The correct thickness of wire, marked on the fuse box, is essential. Should too thick wire be used, the fuse will cease to be a safety device.

Wiring a Lampholder (Fig. 64)

Prepare the ends of the flex by removing half an inch of the cover (a) using a razor blade but taking care not to cut the wires. Thread the flex through the cord grip and lampholder top. Loosen the screws at the terminals; twist the strands of wire tightly together, fold back in half (b), and insert into the lampholder at the terminals, tightening the screws (c). Before screwing down the cover, see that the flex wires are hooked into position according to the design of the lampholder. Binding with thread or insulating tape will prevent friction where the flex enters the lampholder.

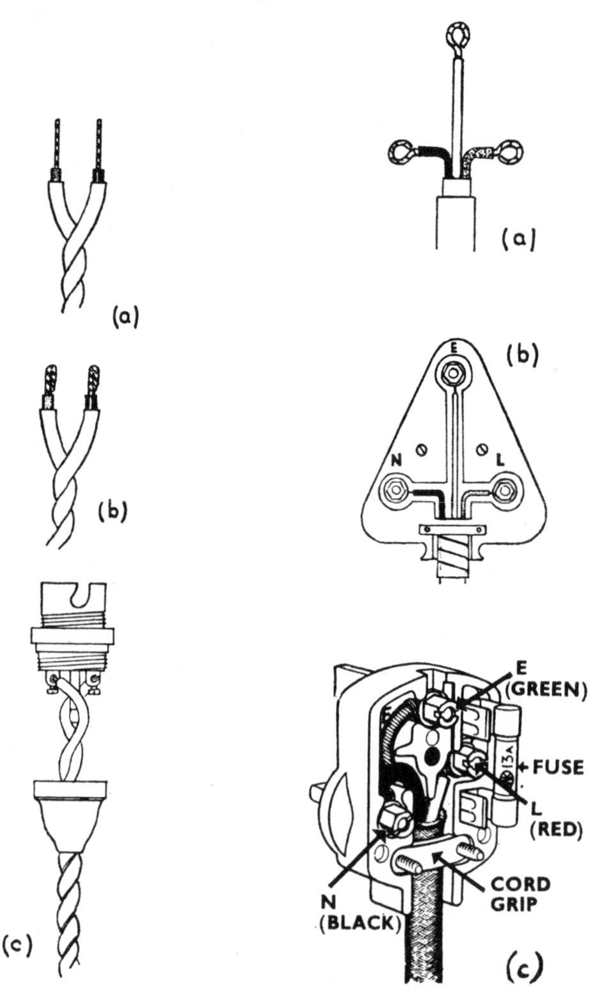

64 *Wiring a lampholder* **65** *Wiring a three-pin plug*

Wiring a Three-pin Plug (Fig. 65)

Cut away about 2 inches of the outer braid covering of the flex and bind the end of the braid with insulating tape to prevent fraying. Fix under the clamp, or cord grip, at the entrance to the plug. Cut each of the three wires so that it is long enough to reach its terminal *plus* an extra half inch for attaching the bared wire. The red wire must be attached to the terminal marked L (live), the black to N (neutral), and the green or brown to the large earth pin terminal marked E (earth). Using a razor blade, remove half an inch of the rubber covering by slitting round carefully and pulling off the rubber; twist the strands of wire firmly together. Then twist the bared section around a screw-driver so that it forms a ring (a) ready to slip over the terminal screw with no stray strands escaping; the direction of the twist should be clockwise. Connect each wire (b) and tighten screws firmly; in each case the rubber should reach practically to the screw. Screw on the top cover of the plug. Exactly the same procedure is followed for a fused plug (c).

Chapter 18

The Management of the Home

AT A TIME of rapid social change, when many factors suggest that family life is declining, it is important to consider the whole question of home life and to decide exactly what contribution a modern housewife may make to society as a whole. Although the old functions of the family, when it was an economic unit and was responsible for many tasks now undertaken by the State, have altered, its basic task is still to serve human needs. Physiological needs may be supplied by a well-run, comfortable home, and for this to be efficiently achieved the house itself must reach a high standard, providing surroundings in every way conducive to good health, easily maintained at a comfortable temperature, with provision for all the work in the house to be done without undue fatigue; there must be sufficient space to give the opportunity for privacy to the inhabitants and for children's play. Houses which fall far below this standard have been seen to have a deleterious effect on the young people growing up within them. In some areas, efforts are being made to build houses designed for families of various sizes and with specific needs; until the necessity for this type of planning is more widely understood, it is inevitable that many of our homes will fall short of this standard.

Yet essential as the satisfaction of the physical needs undoubtedly is, it is only when the young people growing up are given training in responsibility and a sense of purpose and direction, so that they are helped to grow into integrated persons, that the family may be said to be functioning successfully, for only this will enable children to become adjusted to the many social stresses which will be their lot when they leave home. So it is not only the home itself, but its smooth running and the cultivation of good family relationships, which are of vital importance, and as these chiefly devolve upon the housewife, her role is significant and the well-being of her family is very largely in her hands.

In the past, women came to accept that their rightful place was in the home, and in their varying circumstances they adapted their lives accordingly. Where wealth existed and servants were plentiful, their lives were comparatively idle, for they took no positions involving responsibility outside the home, and no part in public affairs. Where means were more limited, they found outlet for their energies in their homes; many became houseproud, spending unlimited and possibly unnecessary time in continual cleaning and polishing; where entertaining took place the preparations for it were elaborate. Since there was nothing labour-saving about the design of many large houses and their equipment, even with the help of servants the housewife's work was full time; with a large family to bring up, she had few interests outside the home and little time for recreation.

The changes in this situation, which began with the twentieth century, were greatly accelerated by two world wars, when women of all classes proved themselves capable of doing men's work in factories and of working alongside them in the Forces. Their status was consequently increased and they earned a new respect. Since the beginning of the century, unmarried women have found both new freedom and interest in offices, where many have reached responsible positions. Improvements in education have enabled them to enter many of the professions, and training has been made available for many occupations which were not formerly thought to require it. With many opportunities continually widening, and training expanding in many directions, the natural development has been that on marriage women have been loath to give up their employment, and many other factors have strengthened their desire to retain it.

The demand for labour has so greatly increased that both unmarried and married women are needed in industry, and married women have little difficulty in finding work of various types within reasonable distance of their homes. Early marriage, small families and increased life span have meant that when their children have reached the age of no longer needing constant attention and care, most women find themselves with over half of their lives still ahead of them. For those who are active and intelligent, the running of a house is not sufficient occupation to be satisfying; many become lonely and bored and long to get out of their homes and meet more people. It is becoming more and more common for young married women to retain outside employment until the arrival of their children, and to return to it when the children have reached school age. For many, of course, the prevalent factor is the economic one; in some cases the extra income is a real necessity, while in others, especially for families who have moved to new estates, it is a means of raising the standard of living for the family until it compares favourably with that of neighbours and friends. For some, it is the means of providing luxuries which in the modern age seem desirable or even essential. In many cases it is understandable that a woman who has been in employment before her marriage looks forward to returning to some degree of financial independence. The fact that many women, both married and unmarried, are now combining two jobs is gaining recognition by employers; standards and conditions of work in factories have improved generally, and in many cases working hours are adapted to suit the particular requirements of married women.

Faced with the two roles which she is expected to play efficiently, a modern housewife discovers the need for organisation and management which, if homes are to be well run and families well cared for, are necessary more than ever before. In the design of modern houses, although many improvements are still necessary, consideration is given to the elimination of fatigue and unnecessary time spent on housework; the small size of house and avoidance of wasted space, the arrangement of the space available and the choice of easily cleaned surfaces all contribute towards smooth running. Newer and more labour-saving equipment for cookery, laundrywork and cleaning appears frequently on the market, and the existence of hire purchase schemes brings it all within the range of smaller income groups.

In industry, the expert study of work processes has resulted in higher efficiency, and less absenteeism on the part of the workers. While similar consideration of the work processes in a home is undoubtedly desirable, there is a danger that too much rigidity may result; where the well being and complete happiness of people are at stake, adaptability is always necessary, even if it entails more time and effort than would appear essential; the very character of a home must not be lost sight of. Nevertheless there must be understanding of the basic factors which help to make work less fatiguing and more enjoyable; good lighting of the work centres, well-designed tools, easy to handle, without any irritating features and kept in good working order, and a comfortable temperature in which to work are obvious necessities. Some knowledge of domestic science is of great advantage to the housewife, for while the numerous scientific developments have resulted in products intended to simplify her work, they may instead, if they are not used intelligently, complicate her life. Unless there is scientific knowledge with which to estimate the accuracy of their assertions, the numerous and constantly increasing advertisements, brought to the housewife's notice in magazines, by television and by pamphlets put through the letter box, may well prove confusing. The modern housewife must keep abreast of developments, but, above all, she needs to have discrimination. Domestic science training gained in her schooldays will stand her in good stead; attendance at adult classes, broadcast talks and feature programmes and articles in good types of women's magazines are all of value.

When time is limited, working to a definite plan is essential; there is indeed little prospect of success without this. The family requires adequate, well-balanced and punctual meals, for which menus must be planned ahead so that shopping may be concentrated into a shorter time. Here the refrigerator is of great assistance. Foods which are packaged, tinned or frozen require little preparation and help to cut down time and also to vary the menus; a good manager will not need to use them to excess. Making full use of the school dinner service and of good canteens which may be available to the workers of the family is advisable; at the same time, the value of meals taken together in the home and as a family should not be ignored. Some at least will be at times of relaxation when the day's work is done and its undertakings ready to be recounted; contributing as it does to the companion aspect of family life, the habit of sharing experiences, particularly satisfying to children, is one to be encouraged.

No longer must the plan of work in a home involve only one worker, a factor which sometimes made a housewife feel a drudge and gave her grounds for self pity, removing all interest and satisfaction from household tasks by the sheer monotony of repetition, and thereby causing additional fatigue. Many modern husbands will enjoy taking some responsibility for the work of a home, and will cheerfully give help with washing up, shopping or even taking washing to the launderette, and looking after children. The many labour-saving materials available, together with the expense saved, have encouraged interest in home decorating. Where daily work in an office or factory may entail little responsibility or skill, the sharing of the work in a home often affords satisfaction, besides being an inevitable result of the wife's employment outside the home.

The allocation of some tasks, preferably those most enjoyed, to the younger members of the family is a good part of the plan from several points of view. It provides opportunity to practise what has been learnt at school, besides giving training in responsibility and unselfishness, which is useful preparation for the future. The provision of sufficient time and good conditions for doing homework must not be interfered with, for, to do well at school, children need help and encouragement at home, and the attitude of their parents may well influence their chances of success. It is found in many families that boys will take as much part in the work of the home as their sisters, doing so with great efficiency and enjoyment; where school time-tables permit, the practice of giving boys the opportunity of domestic science training is proving valuable, and is increasing. To both boys and girls, the acquisition of home skills, and the opportunities to put them into practice in real circumstances, are the parts of their education for which they will be particularly grateful when they have homes of their own.

The habit of discussion in order to make definite plans, drawn up with the purpose of sharing the responsibilities of the home between the husband and wife, should be established right at the beginning of married life. At that time many adjustments are necessary on both sides, and on their success the stability of the marriage largely depends. If the wife is remaining in paid employment it is essential that the husband should, from the beginning, accept and approve of this, adapting his own habits of life in accordance with it. Plans of organisation must be flexible; as the different phases of family life succeed one another, alteration will obviously be necessary. When some or all of the children have grown old enough to take responsibility, they should be included in discussions about the work of the home and encouraged to make suggestions. Encouragement to volunteer for specific tasks will be rewarded by a much more co-operative acceptance of responsibility than if they are imposed by the parents. Plans will obviously differ so greatly according to circumstances that it is impossible to lay down rules; they must take into consideration the work which is necessary daily, the amount to be done at longer intervals, and the special responsibilities undertaken by individuals. The aim must be clearly kept in mind throughout all planning; it will be to accomplish the work efficiently and by the best and quickest methods, so that no one suffers from undue pressure and all have time for relaxation and recreation.

The question of how much entertaining is advisable is of great importance; much is lost if this aspect of family life is ignored or excused on the grounds of lack of time. The household into which even unheralded visitors always feel welcome is not very common but always appreciated, and the housewife who takes unexpected guests in her stride and can welcome them with equilibrium has achieved something of value to herself and to the community. For planned occasions, the elaborate preparations of the past are no longer practicable, nor are they expected; the housewife who is out at work must prepare ahead and gain co-operation of her family, and will succeed in entertaining her friends to meals which are simple but well served in clean and comfortable surroundings. That children enjoy visiting each other's homes is apparent from the fact that on new estates, where grown-ups are inclined to remain aloof from their neighbours, the children are very frequently the instigators in making contact. As they grow up, it is of great importance to them to be able to bring their friends home and to know that they will be welcomed and entertained; again, this provides valuable experience for running their own future homes. Often the modern tendency of young people to spend so much of their leisure time outside their homes could be lessened were greater hospitality extended as a matter of course to their friends, and this factor is a means of strengthening family life.

In all types of entertaining, fuss and worry on the part of the housewife, so easily communicated to the guests, detract from her enjoyment and from theirs. As in everything else, the efficient serving of a meal entails thinking ahead, clearing up as much as possible beforehand to ensure an orderly kitchen, clearing away one course and bringing in the next so calmly and quietly that the conversation is hardly interrupted. And while it is desirable as a general rule to leave washing up until after the departure of the guests, some shy visitors will feel more at home if they are allowed to help.

The leisure activities of her family will usually provide work for the housewife which is additional to her usual routine. Some may be enjoyed as a family, and are always well worth the time and trouble involved in their preparation. Family picnics, especially when some imagination has been employed in preparing the packed meal, are simple pleasures always enjoyed by children; other expeditions undertaken together may have either educational or purely entertainment value. Even in an uncertain climate, the annual holiday is eagerly anticipated for months ahead. Other leisure-time activities in which the children take part are separate from the family, as they follow pursuits for their own age group supplied by Scouts and Guides, youth clubs and the Church; the housewife who takes an interest and gives help where needed is assisting her child's social development and the growth of confidence and security. Contact with the schools, too, is considered to be very desirable, and parent-teacher associations which have been formed have in some areas met with great success. In addition, the housewife must make time to attend school sports days, prize days, open days and entertainments. Provision for hobbies of the various members of a family are difficult to make in a small house. Yet these too are necessary, even though they may cause some inconvenience. From the earliest age, children should be trained to clear up afterwards.

It is obvious that the demands made on a modern housewife are very exacting. Nevertheless, the sense of purpose which she will develop is in itself rewarding. Improved standards and greater comfort in a home may succeed in drawing the family together; where its running becomes a joint enterprise the partnership which is established in the home will strengthen family ties.

MANAGING THE FAMILY INCOME

The budgeting of the family income is an important part of home management, and one about which discussion should take place between the husband and wife at the beginning of their partnership and from time to time as adjustments become necessary. By budgeting is meant the apportioning in advance of parts of the annual income, making sure that all essential items are covered. To do this, complete co-operation between husband and wife is essential, especially where the income is small. If the budgeting is to be of use, account keeping is also necessary; at the end of each year, the budget which was made may be compared with the actual expenditure, and the following year's budget be amended in the light of experience.

It is true that many people find money matters tedious, and to budget and keep accounts requires self-discipline. Much worry and confusion may be avoided by frank discussion and planning ahead. It is a time when there is a strong desire in most people to reach a standard of living which will measure satisfactorily against what is considered more or less normal by the people around them. Advertisements, magazine articles and education on subjects such as nutrition all combine to influence in this direction; easy hire-purchase terms may, to some, be a temptation to spend more than can really be afforded. Even when material possessions are not considered to be the biggest and most important assets to the good life, there is fairly general belief that good standards of housing and home life are desirable, and as income rises, perhaps through the entry of the wife into paid employment, there is a tendency to spend the extra money in the home, on food, clothing, labour-saving devices, adornment in one form or another, and provision for entertainment. This is a good trend provided expenditure is wisely regulated; where it is not, it can lead to disaster.

Details of budgets will obviously vary in different families under different circumstances; the basic items of expenditure will come under the same general headings.

Household Expenses

The main household expenses, forming probably about 45 per cent of the total income, will be in the majority of households in the hands of the wife; she may however prefer her husband to pay fuel and other bills which are conveniently settled by cheque. The largest item of expenditure under this heading will be on food, and the lower the income, the higher the proportion which must be allocated to it if nutritional standards are to be adequate. Education in nutrition forms an important part of home management courses in schools, and is put before the public in various ways so that the diet of the nation may reach an adequate health standard. As a result, it is in most cases the first item to be improved with increased income; better meals are introduced, which are well balanced and use more foods with high protein content and more protective foods. The value of a good, varied diet is understood by the majority of people.

Fuel has become another big item and many will prefer to keep it separate. New equipment for space heating and water heating has been designed with the object of saving fuel, and where possible all obsolete appliances should be replaced. Only by careful consideration of the fuel used in the year is it possible to see whether economies may be effected. Other items under the heading of household expenses will include cleaning materials and laundry.

Housing

In individual budgets, the item which varies most is probably the amount allocated to rent; 20 to 25 per cent is usually suggested to be the maximum proportion advisable. Many will prefer to have much cheaper housing and spend more on luxuries; others will choose to forgo other items which they consider less necessary than satisfactory housing. Careful consideration should be given to the possibility of house purchase, for which the money may be borrowed, and expert advice should be taken before embarking upon it. If the house is owned, annual expenditure under this heading will include interest on mortgage, repayments to a building society, rates, taxes, insurance, repairs and maintenance.

Rates

The general rate, payable half yearly, is a charge calculated at so much in the pound on what is estimated as the rateable value of the house. It is paid to the local authority, and covers services which could not for practical reasons be provided by individuals, such as schools, police, street lighting, refuse collection, sewerage. Water rate is a separate charge, also payable half yearly.

Taxes

Taxes are of two kinds, direct and indirect. The direct tax is levied on income, people earning small incomes being given special concessions. Death duties, the tax paid on the property left behind by people when they die, come under the heading of direct taxation; other taxes are paid in the form of wireless and dog licences. Indirect taxation, which will not appear as a separate item on a budget, is levied on goods and entertainment and is included in the prices paid by the public. Schedule A income tax applies only to people who are buying their own house or already own it. A house returns interest just as any other investment;

if the owner lets it, he receives rent; if he lives in it himself he saves the rent which he would have to pay elsewhere. Schedule A is the tax paid on the income which the house represents.

House Insurance

House insurance must be taken out by people who are buying houses through building societies, insurance companies, etc. and is against damage to the house by fire or other accidents. Furniture should be insured in addition to this. Other policies may be taken out to cover any articles of clothing or jewellery which are of high value, or to cover such articles as television sets.

Clothing

Again, expenditure on this will of necessity vary enormously with circumstances, 10 per cent being suggested as an average. Costs have been kept down to some degree by improved mass production of well-made garments, particularly useful for children's clothing; fewer items are made at home on this account. In the lower income groups, a bigger proportion has often to be allocated to the husband's clothing than to that of the wife; as the income increases, the position is often reversed. Families moved to new estates usually make a special effort to improve the standard of their children's clothing, so that they will not compare unfavourably with other children in school. The cost of commercial cleaning of clothes is usually included under this heading, and in urban areas can be a considerable item.

Savings and Personal Insurances

To this is allocated on an average 5 per cent of the annual income. National insurance is paid by everyone in the country over 15 years of age whose income is more than £140; it is a form of compulsory insurance against unemployment, sickness and other emergencies. Unless other insurance policies are taken out, many people, especially of the lower income groups, find it difficult to meet sudden unexpected expenses. In addition, some form of voluntary saving is always advisable. This may be accomplished by a Post Office Savings Account, which is secure and pays a small rate of interest; it is probably the most advisable method for small savings. The money may be taken out as required, though not withdrawn all at once, except when notice is given. The purchase of National Savings stamps or certificates is another sound method of voluntary saving.

Holidays and Amusements

Every effort should be made to allow an average of 5 per cent of the income for these. Smaller families have resulted in more money being available for leisure; holidays with pay give more opportunities of holidays spent together as a family. The opportunities for holidays for individual members of the family, such as are provided by camps for children of school age, should also be taken where possible.

Incidentals

Under this heading will come fares, subscriptions, presents and all the many small items of this type, which will take about 10 per cent of the income.

As the family grows up, expenditure on the children will obviously increase, and budgets will have to be adjusted accordingly. In a modern industrial society the margin for personal spending is often wider when a young couple marry than later when children arrive without increase in income; for this reason wise budgeting in the early years is essential in order to ensure some saving for the later periods.

The Use of a Bank Account

Two types of bank account are available to the public. The *deposit account* is useful for saving, or for the temporary deposit of capital; interest is paid on the sum deposited; notice must be given before withdrawal. The *current account* is the type most useful to the majority; it may be opened for any sum over £1. No interest is paid on a current account, but the money may be withdrawn at any time during banking hours; charges for keeping the account are usually made according to the number of transactions involved. To open a current account, an interview with the bank manager is required, and a specimen signature must be supplied; the same form of signature should always be used so that the bank officials may recognise it. Statements of account are balanced each day, and the customer may ask for one at any time. Money is withdrawn from a current account by means of a cheque. A cheque is an order in writing by the customer to the bank; it instructs the bank to pay on demand a particular sum, either to a person specified or to the customer himself. To lessen the risk of forgery, printed forms are used for cheques; a government duty of 2*d*. is paid on each cheque. The number of the cheque is stated on it; should it become lost, the bank should be notified in order to stop payment. When a cheque is drawn, the counterfoil should always be filled in, since it supplies a useful record for accounts, and its details may be necessary in order to trace a cheque. To draw a cheque, the date must be filled in in the top right-hand corner. Should it be required to postpone the payment of the sum for some reason, it is possible to post-date the cheque. An antedated cheque will be paid by the bank provided it is not more than six months old; otherwise the bank will require confirmation from the person who wrote it. Next, the name of the payee must be filled in. If the customer wishes to draw out the money for his own use, he may substitute the words "Pay Cash" or "Self" for the name of the payee. The amount of money must be entered on the cheque in words and in figures. Finally, the signature of the drawer must be written in the same form as the specimen supplied to the bank. An open cheque may be cashed across the counter of a bank whose name appears on it.

When posting a cheque, however, it is safer to make use of a crossed cheque. Two parallel lines appear on a crossed cheque, and these may be printed, or drawn in ink; the words "& Co." may appear between them. The crossed cheque instructs the bank to pay the money only into an account and not to hand it across the counter. When the drawer requires the money for his own use, he may write "Pay Cash" between the parallel lines, adding his signature; this converts the cheque into an open one. An extra safeguard is provided by writing the name of the payee's bank, or the words "A/c payee only" between the parallel lines, and some firms request that when cheques are made out to them this should be done.

Open cheques must be endorsed on the back, the endorsement agreeing with the name of the person to whom the cheque is made out, in the same form as on the front of the cheque. If the cheque is made payable to a firm, it may be endorsed by a person appointed to do so, with the words "For and on behalf of". Crossed cheques need no longer be endorsed.

Various other services are undertaken by the bank for its customers. When instructed to do so, the bank will make regular payments on the customer's behalf, and this is useful for premiums payable to an insurance company, for annual subscriptions, etc. Travellers' cheques and foreign currency will be supplied by the bank for travel out of the country. Documents and any other valuables may be deposited into the safe custody of the bank without charge. Dividends on investments, in addition to salaries, may be paid to the bank on a customer's behalf. For a small charge, the bank will take responsibility for a customer's income tax returns and any necessary claims, etc. The bank is always ready to give advice on any financial business if the customer requires it.

APPENDIX

The Educational Aspect of Home Management

EDUCATION FOR FAMILY LIVING has not in this country been given much attention in the past; it is now gradually being realised that the family is the most important form of social life, and that this type of education is essential. In some schools, and in day-continuation classes, efforts are being made to strengthen the status of the family in the minds of youth; in the realms of home decorating and furnishing and labour-saving equipment, every effort is being made to put the idea of a beautiful and simply run home before the public.

It is usually agreed that where conditions make it possible, a practice flat or house should be available for the home management departments in schools, and there is no doubt that where one is in existence and well used, it imparts a reality to the subject which increases its usefulness. In furnishing and equipping the flat, as much as possible should be undertaken by the pupils; both at the beginning and from time to time afterwards, the making of curtains and covers, lampshades, cushions, simple upholstered articles and table linen provides scope for correlation with the art department of the school. Opportunities for practice in home decorating and renovations will occur from time to time. The fullest value will be obtained from the flat by installing groups of pupils to live in it, at least during school hours, for a week or more, giving them responsibility for managing a money allowance, for shopping, for dividing the work of the flat and really running it as a home. The younger members of the family may sometimes be represented by small children "loaned" by a nearby infants school; members of the school staff will usually enjoy being entertained as guests; opportunities for inviting parents may sometimes be given.

The wise use of the school flat gives opportunity for more than the teaching of practical skills; in it the pupils may be helped to realise the underlying aim of accomplishing all the work of a home in such a way that time may be left for leisure; they may be given experience in planning time, in keeping accounts, in planning a scheme of co-operation between various members of a family; they may be helped to develop the poise and self reliance so essential to a housewife in modern society

By testing equipment in use in the flat, they may be helped to develop good judgment in selection.

A boy or girl who has a full and many-sided course in homemaking while at school leaves it with equipment which will help towards living a full life and one which will be useful and satisfying in the community. It is when this goal is understood that the teaching of home management becomes rewarding.

Index

The numerals in **bold** type denote the figure numbers of the illustrations

INDEX